GLOBAL POLITICA

BAHRAIN AND JORDAN
UNREST AND FOREIGN RELATIONS

GLOBAL POLITICAL STUDIES

Additional books in this series can be found on Nova's website under the Series tab.

Additional E-books in this series can be found on Nova's website under the E-books tab.

THE MIDDLE EAST IN TURMOIL

Additional books in this series can be found on Nova's website under the Series tab.

Additional E-books in this series can be found on Nova's website under the E-books tab.

GLOBAL POLITICAL STUDIES

BAHRAIN AND JORDAN

UNREST AND FOREIGN RELATIONS

KEVEN BUCK

AND

TAD J. MCPHERSON

EDITORS

Nova Science Publishers, Inc.

New York

For permission to use material from this book please contact us:
Telephone 631-231-7269; Fax 631-231-8175
Web Site: http://www.novapublishers.com

NOTICE TO THE READER

The Publisher has taken reasonable care in the preparation of this book, but makes no expressed or implied warranty of any kind and assumes no responsibility for any errors or omissions. No liability is assumed for incidental or consequential damages in connection with or arising out of information contained in this book. The Publisher shall not be liable for any special, consequential, or exemplary damages resulting, in whole or in part, from the readers' use of, or reliance upon, this material. Any parts of this book based on government reports are so indicated and copyright is claimed for those parts to the extent applicable to compilations of such works.

Independent verification should be sought for any data, advice or recommendations contained in this book. In addition, no responsibility is assumed by the publisher for any injury and/or damage to persons or property arising from any methods, products, instructions, ideas or otherwise contained in this publication.

This publication is designed to provide accurate and authoritative information with regard to the subject matter covered herein. It is sold with the clear understanding that the Publisher is not engaged in rendering legal or any other professional services. If legal or any other expert assistance is required, the services of a competent person should be sought. FROM A DECLARATION OF PARTICIPANTS JOINTLY ADOPTED BY A COMMITTEE OF THE AMERICAN BAR ASSOCIATION AND A COMMITTEE OF PUBLISHERS.

Additional color graphics may be available in the e-book version of this book.

LIBRARY OF CONGRESS CATALOGING-IN-PUBLICATION DATA

ISBN: 978-1-61942-605-4

Published by Nova Science Publishers, Inc. † New York

CONTENTS

PREFACE

This book examines the political structure, economic, security and U.S. relations with the countries of Bahrain and Jordan. Protests that erupted in Bahrain following the uprising that overthrew Egyptian President Hosni Mubarak on February 11, 2011, demonstrate that Shiite grievances over the distribution of power and economic opportunities were not satisfied by relatively limited efforts to include the Shiite majority in governance. Consequently, several issues in U.S.-Jordanian relations are likely to figure in decisions by Congress and the Administration on future aid to and cooperation with Jordan. These include the stability of the Jordanian regime, the role of Jordan in the Arab-Israeli peace process, the possibility of U.S.-Jordanian nuclear energy cooperation, and U.S.-Jordanian military and intelligence cooperation.

Chapter 1 - Protests that erupted in Bahrain following the uprising that overthrew Egyptian President Hosni Mubarak on February 11, 2011, demonstrate that Shiite grievances over the distribution of power and economic opportunities were not satisfied by relatively limited efforts to include the Shiite majority in governance. Most Sunnis in Bahrain believe the Shiite majority will be satisfied with nothing less than outright rule. As protests escalated in March 2011, Bahrain's government bucked U.S. advice by inviting direct security assistance from other Gulf Cooperation Council countries, declaring a state of emergency, forcefully suppressing demonstrations, and arresting dissident leaders. Although the state of emergency ended on June 1, the continued arrests of dissidents reduced prospects for a negotiated political solution to be achieved in the course of a national dialogue, which began on July 2, 2011, and concluded later that month. The dialogue, harmed by a pullout of the main opposition political society shortly after it began, reached consensus on a few recommendations that did not satisfy the bulk of the Shiite opposition. The main opposition organization also boycotted special parliamentary elections on September 24, 2011, and the boycott widened a sectarian disparity in the elected lower house

Chapter 2 - This chapter provides an overview of Jordanian politics and current issues in U.S.-Jordanian relations. It provides a brief discussion of Jordan's government and economy and of its cooperation in promoting Arab-Israeli peace and other U.S. policy objectives in the Middle East.

Several issues in U.S.-Jordanian relations are likely to figure in decisions by Congress and the Administration on future aid to and cooperation with Jordan. These include the stability of the Jordanian regime, the role of Jordan in the Arab-Israeli peace process, the possibility of U.S.- Jordanian nuclear energy cooperation, and U.S.-Jordanian military and intelligence cooperation.

Although the United States and Jordan have never been linked by a formal treaty, they have cooperated on a number of regional and international issues over the years. The country's small size and lack of major economic resources have made it dependent on aid from Western andfriendly Arab sources. U.S. support, in particular, has helped Jordan address serious vulnerabilities, both internal and external. Jordan's geographic position, wedged between Israel, Syria, Iraq, and Saudi Arabia, has made it vulnerable to the strategic designs of its more powerful neighbors, but has also given Jordan an important role as a buffer between these potential adversaries. In 1990, Jordan's unwillingness to join the allied coalition against Iraq disrupted its relations with the United States and the Persian Gulf states; however, relations improved throughout the 1990s as Jordan played an increasing role in the Arab-Israeli peace process and distanced itself from Saddam Hussein's Iraq.

Chapter 3 - Bahrain is one of the most densely populated countries in the world; about 89% of the population lives in the two principal cities of Manama and Al Muharraq. Approximately 66% of the indigenous population is originally from the Arabian Peninsula and Iran. Bahrain has a sizeable foreign labor force. The government's policies on naturalization remain controversial. In June 2002, the King issued a decree allowing citizens of the Gulf Cooperation Council (GCC) to take up dual Bahraini nationality. Opposition political groups charge that the government is granting citizenship to foreign nationals who have served in the Bahraini armed forces and security services to alter the demographic balance of the country, which is primarily Shi'a. According to passport officials, about 40,000 individuals have been naturalized over the past 50 years (about 10% of the total population).

The indigenous population is 98% Muslim. Although some two-thirds of the indigenous population is Shi'a Muslim, the ruling family and the majority of government, military, and corporate leaders are Sunni Muslims. The small indigenous Christian and Jewish communities make up the remaining 2% of the population. Roughly half of foreign resident community are non-Muslim, and include Christians, Hindus, Baha'is, Buddhists and Sikhs.

Chapter 4 - The land that became Jordan is part of the richly historical Fertile Crescent region. Around 2000 B.C., Semitic Amorites settled around the Jordan River in the area called Canaan. Subsequent invaders and settlers included Hittites, Egyptians, Israelites, Assyrians, Babylonians, Persians, Greeks, Romans, Arab Muslims, Christian Crusaders, Mameluks, Ottoman Turks, and, finally, the British. At the end of World War I, the League of Nations awarded the territory now comprising Israel, Jordan, the West Bank, Gaza, and Jerusalem to the United Kingdom as the mandate for Palestine and Transjordan. In 1922, the British divided the mandate by establishing the semiautonomous Emirate of Transjordan, ruled by the Hashemite Prince Abdullah, while continuing the administration of Palestine under a British High Commissioner. The mandate over Transjordan ended on May 22, 1946; on May 25, the country became the independent Hashemite Kingdom of Transjordan. It ended its special defense treaty relationship with the United Kingdom in 1957.

Transjordan was one of the Arab states which moved to assist Palestinian nationalists opposed to the creation of Israel in May 1948, and took part in the warfare between the Arab states and the newly founded State of Israel. The armistice agreements of April 3, 1949 left Jordan in control of the West Bank and provided that the armistice demarcation lines were without prejudice to future territorial settlements or boundary lines.

In: Bahrain and Jordan   ISBN: 978-1-61942-605-4
Editors: K. Buck and T. J. McPherson   © 2012 Nova Science Publishers, Inc.

Chapter 1

BAHRAIN: REFORM, SECURITY, AND U.S. POLICY[1*]

Kenneth Katzman

SUMMARY

Protests that erupted in Bahrain following the uprising that overthrew Egyptian President Hosni Mubarak on February 11, 2011, demonstrate that Shiite grievances over the distribution of power and economic opportunities were not satisfied by relatively limited efforts to include the Shiite majority in governance. Most Sunnis in Bahrain believe the Shiite majority will be satisfied with nothing less than outright rule. As protests escalated in March 2011, Bahrain's government bucked U.S. advice by inviting direct security assistance from other Gulf Cooperation Council countries, declaring a state of emergency, forcefully suppressing demonstrations, and arresting dissident leaders. Although the state of emergency ended on June 1, the continued arrests of dissidents reduced prospects for a negotiated political solution to be achieved in the course of a national dialogue, which began on July 2, 2011, and concluded later that month. The dialogue, harmed by a pullout of the main opposition political society shortly after it began, reached consensus on a few recommendations that did not satisfy the bulk of the Shiite opposition. The main opposition organization also boycotted special parliamentary elections on

---

[*] This is an edited, reformatted and augmented version of Congressional Research Service Report 95-1013, dated October 18, 2011.

September 24, 2011, and the boycott widened a sectarian disparity in the elected lower house of parliament.

Possibly because of concern that a rise to power of the Shiite opposition could jeopardize the extensive U.S. military cooperation with Bahrain, the Obama Administration has not called for a change of the Al Khalifa regime and continues to meet regime leaders at high levels. Factoring into the U.S. position is a perception in the United States and in the Bahraini government that Iran seeks to take advantage of Shiite unrest in Bahrain to bring a friendly regime to power and reduceU.S. influence in the Persian Gulf. The Administration has criticized governmental use of force and widescale arrests of peaceful protesters and urged further reform, but these criticisms have been insufficient to satisfy those who believe the United States is treating Bahrain differently than it has other Middle East cases in 2011.

The U.S.-Bahrain security relationship is deep and long-standing. In exchange for a tacit security guarantee against Iran or other aggressors, Bahrain has provided key support for U.S. interests by hosting U.S. naval headquarters for the Gulf for over 60 years and by providing facilities and small numbers of personnel for U.S. war efforts in Iraq and Afghanistan. Because of the instability in Bahrain, there is concern that U.S. use of the naval headquarters facilities might become untenable, but there are no evident moves to relocate it. This facility has been pivotal to U.S. strategy to deter any Iranian aggression as well as to interdict the movement of terrorists and weapons-related technology on Gulf waterways. Beyond the naval facility, the United States signed a formal defense pact with Bahrain in 1991 and has designated Bahrain as a "major non- NATO ally," entitling it to sales of sophisticated U.S. weapons systems. Bahrain also receives small amounts of U.S. security assistance. New U.S. sales and aid are coming under criticism from human rights and other groups; legislation has been introduced opposing a U.S. equipment sale announced in September 2011. On regional issues such as the Arab-Israeli dispute, Bahrain has tended to defer to Saudi Arabia or other powers to take the lead in formulating proposals or representing the position of the Persian Gulf states, collectively.

Fueling Shiite unrest is the fact that Bahrain, having largely run out of crude oil reserves, is poorer than most of the other Persian Gulf monarchies. The country has tried to compensate through diversification, particularly with banking and some manufacturing. In September 2004, the United States and Bahrain signed a free trade agreement (FTA); legislation implementing it was signed January 11, 2006 (P.L. 109-169). The unrest in 2011 has further strained Bahrain's economy.

THE POLITICAL STRUCTURE, REFORM, AND HUMAN RIGHTS[1]

The Al Khalifa family, which is Sunni Muslim and generally not as religiously conservative as the leaders of neighboring Saudi Arabia, has ruled Bahrain since 1783. The Al Khalifa family's arrival from the Saudi peninsula to take control ended a century of domination by Persian settlers. The Al Khalifa subsequently received political protection from Britain, which was the dominant power in the Gulf until the early 1970s. Bahrain became independent from Britain in August 1971 after a 1970 U.N. survey (some refer to its as a "referendum") determined that its inhabitants preferred independence to Iranian control.

Bahrain is led by King Hamad bin Isa Al Khalifa (about 61 years old), who succeeded his father, Shaykh Isa bin Sulman Al Khalifa, upon his death in March 1999. Educated at Sandhurst Military Academy in Britain, King Hamad was previously commander of the Bahraini Defense Forces (BDF). His son, Shaykh Salman bin Hamad, about 41 years old, is Crown Prince. Shaykh Salman is U.S.-and U.K.-educated and, like the King, has long been considered a proponent of reformand accommodation with Bahrain's Shiite majority—about 60%-70% of the 503,000-person citizenry.[2] (There are an estimated 235,000 expatriates in Bahrain, according to the Central Intelligence Agency's *World Factbook* July 2010 estimate.) About 25% of the population is age 14 or younger.

To preserve its power, the Al Khalifa family has insisted on holding onto all strategic ministry positions and at least half of all ministerial slots. Even before the unrest that has seen most senior Shiites in government resign, there were only four Shiite ministers out of 23 cabinet positions (plus one out of the four deputy prime ministers), and those ministries run by Shiites have been considered less critical. Shiites are also highly underrepresented in the security forces, serving mainly in administrative tasks.

The King's uncle (the brother of the late ruler), Prime Minister Khalifa bin Salman Al Khalifa, along with other Sunni hard-liners including Minister of the Royal Court Khalid bin Ahmad bin Salman Al Khalifa[3] and Interior Minister Rashid bin Abdullah Al Khalifa, have always been skeptical of King Hamad's reforms. They believe that the concessions that King Hamad made to the Shiite majority prior to the 2011 unrest caused the Shiites to increase their political demands rather than satisfy them. Others believe that level of unrest reached in February 2011 would have been reached long ago had the King's reforms not been enacted.

King Hamad's reforms, although judged minor by the Shiite majority, are far more extensive than those made by his father Amir Isa during his rule. In December 1992, Amir Isa established a 30- member appointed Consultative Council to comment on proposed laws. In June 1996, he expanded it to 40 members. These reforms did not come close to quieting the demands of either Shiites or Sunnis for the restoration of an elected national assembly, even though Bahrain's Sunnis are considered less hungry for "democracy" than are the Shiites. An elected assembly was provided for under the 1973 constitution but abolished in August 1975 because of fear of sectarian competition and tensions over control of the body. In the years just prior to Shaykh Hamad's accession to rulership, there was daily anti-government violence during 1994-1998, although the unrest gradually took on a Shiite sectarian character.

As Hamad's first reform steps after taking over, he changed his title to "King," rather than "Amir" and implying more accountability, and held a referendum (February 14, 2002) on a new "National Action Charter (constitution)." However, the Shiite majority population criticized the National Action Charter because it established that the elected Council of Rep-resentatives (COR) and the all-appointed *Shura* (Consultative) Council were to be of equal size (40 seats each). Together, they constitute a National Assembly (parliament) that serves as a partial check on government power. The King, through the prime minister, makes all cabinet appointments and thus exercises direct rule; the Assembly does not appoint—or have power to reject—cabinet appointments.

The COR can propose (but not actually draft) legislation and both chambers can question ministers, although not in public session. The COR can, by a two-thirds majority, vote noconfidence against ministers and the prime minister and override the King's veto of approved legislation, although none of these actions has occurred since the COR was formed. The King has the authority to dissolve the COR and amend the constitution. The Shura Council is formally limited to amending draft legislation and, in concert with the COR, reviewing the annual budget, but these powers provide the Shura Council with the ability to block action by the COR. The government has tended to appoint generally more educated and pro-Western members to the Shura Council, and it is generally more supportive of the government than is the elected COR. There is no "quota" for females in the National Assembly, as has been included in democratic constitutions in post-Saddam Iraq and post-Taliban Afghanistan.

The National Assembly has tended to address primarily economic and social issues, and not national security issues. For example, in May 2010, it voted to ban sale of alcohol to Muslims, although subject to implementing regulations made by the King, through the government. Other legislation considered in the Bahraini National Assembly in recent years included bills to combat cyber crime, regulate the pharmaceutical sector, regulate the press, create an anti-corruption body, and establish a higher council on social security. However, many of these bills stalled in the 2006- 2010 parliament due to lack of consensus and broader Sunni-Shiite tensions.

Post-Charter Elections

Elections have been held every four years since 2002, each time marked by substantial tension between the government and the Shiite majority. Formal political parties are banned, but factions compete as "political societies" which serve as the functional equivalent of parties for election purposes. In the COR elections, if no candidate in a contested district wins more than 50% in the first round, a runoff is held one week later.

2002 Elections
The first elections under the Charter were held in October 2002. In the 2002 election, many Shiite opposition "political societies," including Al *Wifaq*, (formally, the Al *Wifaq* National Islamic Society, also known as the Islamic National Accord Association—a large faction, led by Shaykh Ali al-Salman), boycotted the elections on the grounds that setting the COR and the Shura Council at the same size dilutes popular will. The 2002 boycott lowered turnout (about 52%) and helped Sunnis win two-thirds of the COR seats. Of the 170 total candidates, six were women, but none of the women were elected.

2006 Elections
As was widely expected by experts, Sunni-Shiite tensions escalated again in the run-up to the November 25, 2006, parliamentary and municipal elections. The tension was aggravated by the Shiite perception that a once-repressed Shiite majority came to power in Iraq through U.S.- backed elections and that the Bahraini majority was entitled to a similar result. In the fall of 2006, some Shiites protested, particularly after allegations, some of which were publicly corroborated by a government adviser (Salah al-Bandar) in

August 2006 in a report to an outside human rights organization, that the government was adjusting election districts so as to favor Sunni candidates. It was also alleged that the government issued passports to Sunnis in an attempt to shift the demographic balance to the Sunnis' advantage.

In the November 2006 elections, two Shiite opposition blocs, *Wifaq* and the National Democratic Action Association, participated, raising voter turnout to 72%. *Wifaq* is avowedly Islamist in political orientation. A harder-line Shiite opposition faction, *Al Haq* (Movement of Freedom and Democracy), boycotted. The opposition, led by *Wifaq,* won 17 seats, virtually all those it contested. The Shiite opposition was therefore the largest single bloc in the COR, but it was short of a majority.

The government was heartened that Sunni Muslims won 23 total seats. Of those, eight were won by secular Sunnis and 15 were won by Islamist Sunnis (eight from the Salafists trend and seven Muslim Brotherhood members). Only one woman (Latifa al Qaoud, who was unopposed in her district) won, out of 18 female candidates (down from 31 female candidates in the 2002 elections). As evidence of continued friction, *Wifaq* boycotted the speakership contest, and incumbent COR Speaker Khalifa al-Dhahrani was reelected speaker.

The King subsequently named a new Shura Council with 20 Shiites, 19 Sunnis, and one Christian (a female). Ten women were appointed. However, the Shiites appointed were not all aligned with opposition factions, and several were considered "pro-government." Therefore, the Shura Council was not a bastion of opposition to the government even though Shiites held half of its seats. In a nod to the increased Shiite strength as a result of the elections, the government appointed a Shiite (Jawad al-Araidh) as one of the four deputy prime ministers and another (who is close to *Wifaq*) as a minister of state for foreign affairs. Three other Shiites remained in the cabinet.

Heightened political tensions continued in between national elections. In December 2008, the government made numerous arrests of Shiite demonstrators and accused some of being part of a foreign-inspired "plot" to destabilize Bahrain. Some were accused of undergoing guerrilla or terrorist training in Syria. On January 26, 2009, the government arrested three leading Shiite activists, including the wheelchair-bound Dr. Abduljalil Alsingace and Mr. Hassan Mushaima, both leaders of *Al Haq.* They were tried during February-March 2009 but, along with other Shiite activists, were pardoned and released in April 2009. Alsingace has visited the United States several times to highlight the human rights situation in Bahrain. (As noted below, Alsingace was arrested again in August 2010. Mushaima subsequently went into exile in

Europe. Mushaima was arrested after his return and both are on trial in connection with the 2011 unrest.)

The 2010 National Assembly and Municipal Election: Prelude to the Uprising

The resentments over the 2006 election, and the still unfulfilled demand of Bahrain's Shiites for greater political power and an end to economic discrimination, carried over to the 2010 election. The election was held on October 23, 2010, with a second round runoff for some districts on October 30. There were only a limited number of international observers, primarily from various international human rights organizations. Two Bahraini human rights watchdog groups, the Bahrain Human Rights Society and the Bahrain Transparency Society, again (for the third time) reached agreement to jointly monitor the 2010 elections. Municipal elections were held concurrently.

The electorate was about 300,000 persons, voting in 40 districts spread throughout five governorates. As was the case in the 2006 elections, Shiite oppositionists accused the government of drawing district boundaries so as to prevent the election of a Shiite majority. Registration of candidates took place during September 12-16, 2010. About 200 people registered to run, of whom seven were women. However, one woman withdrew after registering, leaving a field of six female candidates. Of the six, only one was formally endorsed by a political society, the leftleaning, nonsectarian National Democratic Action Society (*Waad*, which means "promise" in Arabic). She is Munira Fakhro, a prominent Shiite woman who was exiled prior to the political reform process begun by King Hamad. In 2006, she narrowly lost to a Sunni Islamist (*Minbar*, or "platform," faction). At least four candidates in districts where there was no opposition were declared winners by September 28, 2010. One of them was a *Wifaq* member.

Wifaq, still by far the most prominent Shiite political society, fielded candidates. Its leader, Shaykh Ali Salman, was not a candidate, preferring to continue to lead the faction from the background. *Al Haq* again boycotted, as it did in 2006. In the run-up to the election, the government cracked down on Shiite activitists, particularly those who supported boycotting the election. For example, on September 4, 2010, 23 Shiite leaders were arrested on charges of attempting a violent overthrow of the government. They were among about 160 Shiites arrested in August and September, under a 2006 anti-terrorism law that gives the government broad arrest and prosecution powers. Among those arrested was Dr. Alsingace (see above), on August 13, 2010, upon his return from abroad. Alsingace remained incarcerated and told his lawyers that he was being beaten and deprived of sleep. A prominent Shiite cleric, Ayatollah Hussein Mirza al- Najati, said to be close to the most senior Iraqi cleric Ayatollah Ali al-Sistani, had his Bahraincitizenship revoked on September 20, 2010.

Some observers asserted that the government crackdown would drive Bahraini Shiites to politically support boycotting harder-line movements, such as *Al Haq*, and in so doing suppress the election turnout among Shiites. The crackdown did not prompt *Wifaq* to reverse its decision to compete. The crackdown might have helped the government's election strategy but it also led to stepped up demonstrations by Shiite youth in Shiite neighborhoods. The tensions are also widely blamed for resulting in a bombing that damaged four police cars on September 15, 2010. The tensions over the election almost certainly were a catalyst for the major unrest that has occurred in February 2011, discussed further below.

Among Sunni political societies, there are two that are considered Islamist. They include Minbar, mentioned above, which is an offshoot of the Muslim Brotherhood, and Al Asala, which is a harder-line "Salafist" political society. As noted below, in the 2006-2010 parliament, Asala and Minbar members held a combined 15 seats.

2010 Election Results

Despite the pre-election tensions, the election was held without major reports of violence. Turnout was about 67% between the two rounds. The results, some unexpected, included

- The increase of *Wifaq's* representation from 17 seats in the 2006-2010 COR to 18 seats. However, 18 is still short of a majority.
- Unexpected losses by Sunni Islamist factions, reducing their total to five seats from 15. Minbar and Asala each saw dramatic reductions in their seats from 2006: Minbar (Muslim Brotherhood) decreased to two seats (from seven) and Asala decreased to three seats (from eight). Most of the seats were picked up by Sunni independents, who won 17 seats, up from nine in the 2006-2010 parliament. In addition, the secular and generally leftwing ideological Waad won no seats at all. These results appeared to represent a rejection of Islamist ideology, and even all ideological candidates, in favor of pragmatists who would address Bahrain's economic difficulties.

- The same one woman won who had won in 2006.
- In the municipal elections conducted concurrently, one woman was elected in the second round—the first woman to be elected to a municipal council.

In advance of the December 14, 2010, start of the parliamentary term, the King named the 2010- 2014 Shura Council. Thirty of the 40 serving Council members were reappointed, leaving only 10 newly appointed members. A total of 19 Shiites were appointed, including the speaker. The Council has four women, substantially fewer than the 2006-2010 Council that had nine women. Among the four, one is Jewish (Nancy Khadouri), out of a Jewish population in Bahrain of about 40 persons, and one is Christian (Hala Qarrisah). Bahrain has an estimated 1,000 Christians. The Council speaker, Ali al-Salih, a Shiite, was reappointed.

Table 1. Comparative Composition of National Assembly

	2006	2010	Post-By-Election (October 2011)
Council of Representatives (COR)			
Wifaq (Shiite Islamist)	17	18	0
Shiite Independent	0	0	8
Sunni Independent (mostly secular) in COR	8	17	27
Moderate Sunni Islamist (Minbar, Muslim Brotherhood)	7	2	2
Conservative Sunni Islamist (Asala, Salafi)	8	3	3
	2006	2010	(October 2011)
COR Sect Composition	23 Sunni, 17 Shiite	22 Sunni, 18 Shiite	32 Sunni, 8 Shiite
Women in COR	1	1	4
Shura Council (Upper House, appointed)			
Sectarian, Religious Composition Upper House (Shura Council)	20 Shiite, 19 Sunni, 1 Christian	19 Shiite, 19 Sunni, 1 Christian, 1 Jew	Same as before
Number of Women	9	4	same

2011 Uprising

King Hamad's efforts to accommodate Shiite aspirations were demonstrated to have failed when a major uprising began on February 14, 2011, in the wake of the success of an uprising in Egypt that forced the resignation of Egyptian President Hosni Mubarak. After a few days of protests and relatively minor confrontations with the mostly Bahraini Sunni and expatriate Sunni security forces, the mostly Shiite demonstrators converged on the interior of a major traffic circle, "Pearl Roundabout," named after a statue that depicted Bahrain's pearl-diving past. The uprising tookplace after King Hamad had authorized the latest annual iteration of a $2,700 payment to citizens. The initial demands of the protesters were numerous, but generally centered on such political reforms as altering the constitution to expand the powers of the COR; ending gerrymandering that prevents Shiites from winning a majority in the COR; providing more jobs and economic opportunities; and, among some protesters, replacing hard-line Prime Minister Khalifa. A consistent theme among protesters appeared to be to end the sense among Shiites that they are "second class citizens" or "not trusted" as Bahraini citizens. On February 15, 2011, King Hamad spoke to the nation and announced the formation of a committee to investigate the use of force against protestors, which had killed two until that time.

The unrest took on new dimensions in the early morning of February 17, 2011, when security forces surrounded the thousands of demonstrators in Pearl Roundabout, many of whom were asleep, and used rubber bullets and tear gas to remove them from the location. At least four demonstrators were killed; others died subsequently. The government asserted it had warned of the impending move, an account disputed by the protesters. At a news conference later on February 17, Foreign Minister Khalid Al Khalifa claimed that the Pearl Roundabout was cleared to avoid a "sectarian abyss"—all-out civil conflict between the Shiites and Sunnis. Despite heavy security patrols, additional protests took place on February 18, 2011, and security forces apparently shot several demonstrators. Politically, *Wifaq* pulled all 18 of its deputies out of the COR immediately following the February 17 crackdown. Britain closed its embassy in Bahrainafter the February 17, 2011, crackdown, and announced it might ban further arms exports toBahrain.

Government Tactics Change, As Do Protester Demands

In part at the reported urging of the United States, the government changed tactics on February 19, 2011, pulling security forces back from confronting protesters. That day, demonstrators re-entered Pearl Roundabout and held large demonstrations at or around that location subsequently. A February 22, 2011, demonstration was said to be perhaps the largest in Bahrain's history, although some accounts say that a demonstration three days later, which spanned miles of downtown roads, was even larger. The February 22 demonstration followed by one day a largecounter-demonstration by mostly Sunni supporters of the government.

At the same time, the government, with Crown Prince Salman leading the effort, invited the representatives of the protesters to begin a formal dialogue to try to agree on reforms. That effort was supported by a gesture by King Hamad on February 22, 2011, to release or pardon 308 Bahrainis, including the exiled leader of the hardline *Al Haq*, Hassan Mushaima (who returned to Bahrain from exile in Europe on February 27, 2011). According to the government, these persons were tried not for political views, per se, but rather for committing or advocating violence. On February 26, 2011, King Hamad changed several cabinet posts; this included dropping two Al Khalifa family members from the cabinet. The posts changed were those that can influence job opportunities and living conditions.

The pulling back of the security forces, offers of dialogue, and the cabinet reshuffles did not prevent the protesters' demands from escalating or cause them to leave Pearl Roundabout. The government concessions exposed long-standing splits in the opposition, such as that between the more moderate *Wifaq* and the more hardline *Al Haq*. Anger at the government's initial use of force appeared to shift many demonstrators closer to *Al Haq*, which, as of the beginning of March 2011, demanded a resignation of the monarchy outright. *Wifaq* and other more moderate groups appeared willing to accept the formation of a constitutional monarchy, as discussed further below, and efforts to promote more job opportunities for Shiites. Six smaller hardline Shiite political societies reportedly joined *Al Haq* in insisting on maximalist demands.[4] The regime's offer of dialogue was not taken up consistently or systematically by the more moderate groups, and only informal meetings took place in search of a political solution.

The Saudi/GCC Intervention and Crackdown

With no systematic dialogue begun, protests escalated. On March 1, 2011, demonstrators blocked the entrance to the parliament building and delayed the meeting of its bodies for six hours. The protests also began to spark Sunni-Shiite clashes which some Bahrainis believed were evolving into outright sectarian conflict at the mass level—whereas previously sectarianism had been a concept mainly confined to power struggles among the elites. On March 13, 2011, protesters blockaded the financial district of the capital, Manama, prompting governmental fears that the unrest could choke this major economic sector. Security forces were overwhelmed.

On March 13, Bahrain requested that the Gulf Cooperation Council (GCC), of which it is a member, send additional security forces to protect key sites. In response to the request, on March 14, 2011, a GCC force (from the GCC joint Peninsula Shield unit) spearheaded by a reported 1,200 Saudi forces (in 20 tanks and in other armored vehicles) and 600 UAE police crossed into Bahrain and took up positions at key locations in and around Manama. Kuwait sent naval forces to help Bahrain secure its maritime borders. On March 15, 2011, King Hamad declared a threemonth state of emergency technically headed by BDF Chief of Staff Marshal Khalifa bin Ahmad Al Khalifa, and Bahraini security forces, freed up by the GCC deployment, cleared demonstrators from Pearl Roundabout (and demolished the pearl monument itself on March 18, 2011).[5] Some additional protester deaths were reported in this renewed crackdown. In conjunction, seven Shiite leaders were arrested, including *Al Haq*'s Mushaima. *Wifaq*'s leader, Shaykh Ali Salman, was not arrested. The remaining Shiite ministers in the cabinet, many of the Shiites in the Shura Council, and many Shiites in other senior posts in the judiciary and elsewhere resigned, although a few subsequently returned to service.

Well before intervening in Bahrain, the GCC states had begun to fear that the Bahrain unrest could spread to other GCC states. It was also feared that Iran might be able to exploit the situation. None of the other GCC states has a Shiite majority (like Bahrain), but most of them, including Saudi Arabia, have substantial Shiite minorities. The GCC states met at the foreign minister level on February 16, 2011, and expressed solidarity with the government of Bahrain. King Hamad visited Saudi Arabia on February 23, 2011, for consultations on how to handle the unrest, and Crown Prince Salman visited UAE on March 2, 2011. Those countries have arranged for large pledges of aid (some reports mention $20 billion) to help the Bahrain government (and that of Oman, which also has faced unrest) create jobs for Shiites. Some warned that Saudi intervention would prompt a wider conflict by prompting Iranian intervention on the side of the Shiite protesters. Allegations of Iranian involvement in the unrest are discussed later in the section on Bahrain's foreign policy.

Post-GCC Intervention Situation/End of State of Emergency

Most public protests ceased subsequent to the GCC intervention, although some, mostly neighborhood-based demonstrations continue despite a heavy security force presence around Manama. Human rights groups, including those testifying at a May 13, 2011, hearing of the Tom Lantos Human Rights Commission, reported a broad crackdown in which hundreds were in detention, including at least 50 medical professionals who helped tend to injured protestors. Over 1,500 people, mostly Shiites, had been dismissed from their jobs, although labor movement officials say the figure exceeds 2,600. To date, according to Bahraini government figures, 30 Bahraini protesters have died in the violence, although opposition figures are much higher. Some sources say the government bulldozed about 30 Shiite mosques as a measure to prevent Shiites from gathering.

Prominent Dissidents Arrested

As part of what U.S. officials and many observers called an excessive crackdown, in early April 2011, the government closed the pro-opposition newspaper *Al Wasat*; it editor-in-chief, Mansour al-Jamri, went on trial on May 18, 2011, for inciting violence. A well-known human rights activist, Bahrain Center for Human Rights founder Abdul Hadi al-Khawaja, was arrested April 9, 2011, and his daughter, Maryam, subsequently undertook a hunger strike. On April 15, 2011, the government announced that *Wifaq* and another Shiite political society, the Islamic Action Association, were being investigated for harming national unity and could potentially be disbanded. On May 2, 2011, two *Wifaq* officials who had resigned from the COR because of the unrest, Matar Matar and Jawad Fairuz, were arrested. On May 8, 2011, 14 oppositionists, including Mushaima and Alsingace, went on trial before a state security court; seven others went on trial in absentia. On June 23, 2011, Mushaima, Alsingace, and six other hardline Shiite leaders were sentenced to life in prison.[6] On May 31, a key activist, the head of the Bahrain Center for Human Rights, Nabeel Rajab, was summoned before the military court prosecuting alleged agitators. On June 6, 2011, 47 doctors and nurses were put on trial for aiding protesters.

On September 29, 2011, 20 medical personnel were sentenced by a military court to jail time ranging from five to 15 years, a sentence harshly criticized by human rights activists worldwide. The government said the sentences were not for helping protesters medically, but for inciting sectarian hatred, possession of illegal weapons, and forcibly occupying a public building. Following international criticism, on October 5, 2011, the government announced they would be retried in a civilian court.

Perceiving the regime had gained the upper hand, the King announced in early May that the state of emergency would end on June 1, two weeks earlier than scheduled. The government held to that schedule; the GCC forces that deployed to Bahrain, including the Kuwaiti naval force, began to depart in late June 2011. The departures are believed to have been complete, although some oppositionists assert that some GCC forces remain as of October 2011. King Hamad spoke to the population on May 31 to mark the end of the emergency, offering unconditional dialogue with the opposition beginning July 1, 2011.

Commission of Inquiry Formed

On June 29, 2011, as a further gesture toward the opposition, the King of a five-person "Bahrain Independent Commission of Inquiry," (BICI) headed by Dr. Cherif Bassiouni, to investigate the government's response to the unrest that began in February, and to file its report by October 30, 2011. It held a public forum on July 24, but has come under criticism from Shiite opposition figures who have interpreted certain Bassiouni statements as a bias in favor of exonerating top government officials and blaming human rights abuses on lower level security officers.

National Dialogue and Results

The "National Dialogue" began on July 2, 2011, under the chairmanship of speaker of the COR Dhahrani. with about 300 delegates, of which the Shiite opposition had 35-50 delegates. Of those, five belonged to *Wifaq*.[7] The dialogue, which was to last several weeks, addressed political, economic, social, and human rights issues; each had 15 sub-themes and each sub-theme has 90 topics. Senior Bahraini officials said the intent of the dialogue was to outline a vision of Bahrain rather than necessarily reach agreement on specific steps. After extensive internal debate, *Wifaq* accepted the offer to participate in the dialogue. Its decision may have been prompted by the government's release, a few days prior of about 150 of those who had been imprisoned for the unrest.

Outcomes of the National Dialogue were difficult to predict. Many in the opposition maintained that the continuing detention of many oppositionists did not augur well for progress. The prospects further diminished on July 18, 2011, when *Wifaq,* which had always asserted that it would pull out of the talks if and when it became clear that its proposals for a fully elected parliament with legislative powers would not be met, announced its withdrawal.

That major step built on an earlier decision by the group on July 7, 2011, to cease participating in the economic and social issues meetings. Others took note of the fact that the Crown Prince, the principal champion of dialogue within the upper ranks of the regime, did not chair the dialogue. This suggests he remains in eclipse by harder line Al Khalifa members allied with the prime minister.

The dialogue concluded in late July 2011 after reaching consensus on a few recommendations, which were endorsed by the government on July 29. That day, an unknown number of Shiite demonstrators held a licensed demonstration, but an attempt to march on the U.S. Embassy in Manama was reportedly blocked by security forces.

The core of the recommendations were:

- an elected parliament (lower house) with expanded powers, including: the power to confirm or reject a nominated cabinet, the power to confirm or veto the government's four year work plan, the right to discuss any agenda item, and the power to question ministers on their performance or plans. In addition, the Chairman of the National Committee that presides over the National Assembly should be derived from among the elected COR, not the Shura Council.
- a government "reflecting the will of the people."
- "fairly" demarcated electoral boundaries.
- reworking of laws on naturalization and citizenship.
- combating financial and administrative corruption.
- efforts to reduce sectarian divisions and to fairly.
- There were reportedly 82 economic recommendations, including new mechanisms to provide food subsidies to only the most needy citizens. The government subsequently appointed a committee to implement the recommendations, headed by former Foreign Minister and now deputy Prime Minister Muhammad Mubarak Al Khalifa. He and other officials conducted rounds of meetings with both houses of the National Assembly and with government ministries to begin implementation.

For the opposition, the National Dialogue was largely a failure. The Dialogue did not endorse the ideas of *Wifaq* and other groups proposals for a fully elected parliament with legislative powers, or for the direct selection of the prime minister by the largest coalition in the elected legislature. *Wifaq* was unsatisfied that the Dialogue did not endorse reducing the size and powers of the appointed Shura Council, or the specific pledge to redraw electoral boundaries. To the opposition, the lack of such a pledge signals that the government will continue to gerrymander districts to ensure a Sunni majority in the lower house.

Nor did the opposition achieve other gains, either as a result of the Dialogue or separately. A widely discussed interim compromise has been the replacement of Prime Minister Khalifa, who is widely despised by the opposition, with *Wifaq* leader Shaykh Ali Salman or another moderate opposition figure. The government has not agreed to this step even though, throughout the crisis, some Bahrainis have said that the dismissal of Prime Minister Khalifa Al Khalifa, was likely.[8] Another interim compromise, not adopted to date, could include a broad reshuffling of the cabinet to give Shiites many more ministerial posts and control of key economic ministries. *Wifaq* already holds the majority of seats on several elected municipal councils, although these bodies do not have national legislative authority.

Widespread Shiite demonstrations did not erupt after the conclusion of the Dialogue, although a youth was killed by security forces at one protest on August 31, 2011. In part as a gesture of reconciliation after the Dialogue concluded, on August 8 the government released the two jailed Wifaq COR deputies Matar and Fairuz, along with several other jailed activists. In a speech on August 28, 2011, near the conclusion of the holy month of Ramadan, King Hamad announced the pardoning of some protesters, and the reinstatement of some of the approximately 2,700 of those who had been fired for alleged participation in unrest.

Some believe the GCC intervention and subsequent crackdown hardened Shiite demands to the point where implementation of the national dialogue consensus recommendations will be dismissed and any further compromise is difficult. Harder line Shiite groups believe that no compromise is possible with the Al Khalifa regime still in power, and that increased protests and actions intended to collapse the economy will force the government to fall. The overthrow of the government and the ascension of a Shiite-led regime is possible, although the GCC determination to prevent this makes this outcome less likely, at least in the short term. On the regime side, compromise has been made more difficult by the apparent political eclipse of the Crown Prince, who favors dialogue and negotiation, and the ascendancy within the regime of the prime minister and other hardliners.

September 24-October 1 Special Election

Although activists say demonstrations take place in Shiite villages every night, the main commercial areas of Bahrain remained mostly calm from the time of the national dialogue untilthe special elections to fill the seats vacated by the 18 *Wifaq* COR deputies that had resigned at the outset of the unrest. The elections were scheduled for September 24, 2011, with a second round to be held on October 1, if needed. However, the legitimacy of the special elections was clouded by the announcement by *Wifaq* on August 14, 2011, that it would boycott the elections. That position was based on Wifaq's decision that the national dialogue's reform recommendations were not sufficiently extensive. Several anti-government demonstrations took place in the run-up to the elections and on the days of the election, mostly in Shiite neighborhoods.

In advance of the elections, four winners were declared (including one woman) because they were running unopposed. In both rounds of voting, turnout was assessed as very low, at about 20%, although the government put out official turnout figures of close to 50%. After the first round on September 24, five additional seats were decided. The October 1 runoff decided the remaining nine seats. As shown in Table 1, of the 18 seats decided in the special election, 10 were won by Sunnis, largely because of the *Wifaq* boycott and low turnout. This suggests that most Shiites viewed the special election as illegitimate, but the net result is that Sunnis now overwhelmingly dominate the COR, with 32 seats to only eight Shiite seats. The special election resulted in the addition of three women COR deputies.

The next major benchmark in the unrest and the Bahraini response will be the release of the Independent Commission of Inquiry report by October 30.

U.S. Posture on the Uprising

The U.S. response to the unrest in Bahrain has been colored by the vital U.S. security interests in Bahrain. The U.S. concern is that a fall of the Al Khalifa regime and ascension of a Shiite-led government could increase Iran's influence and lead to an unwanted loss of the U.S. use of Bahrain's military facilities. The seeming priority of these considerations to U.S. officials have prompted criticism from human rights organizations, Bahrain's opposition, and other regional governments that the United States applies different standards in its response to unrest in allied countries such as Bahrain than it does to countries in which a change of regime might not harm U.S. interests, such as Libya or Syria.

The Administration has stressed that it has been highly critical of Bahrain's use of force against protesters. In phone calls to their counterparts after the February 17, 2011, clearing of Pearl Roundabout, Secretary of State Clinton and Secretary of Defense Gates reportedly expressed concern to the Bahrain government for using force against the protesters. These contacts reportedly contributed to the government decision to exercise restraint at that time.

Just prior to the GCC intervention and subsequent crackdown, Secretary of State Clinton and other U.S. officials had praised the release of political prisoners and called on all parties to take up the offer by the Crown Prince for a broad political dialogue on reform.[9] In a statement, President Obama praised the February 26 cabinet reshuffle and King Hamad's restatements of his commitment to reform.[10]

The U.S. position did not change substantially following the GCC intervention, but the United States did become somewhat more critical as the subsequent crackdown proceeded. U.S. officials expressed the view that the crackdown would further inflame unrest over the long term, rather than achieve quiescence and stability. On March 19, 2011, Secretary Clinton reiterated the U.S. support for the Crown Prince's offer of dialogue, and said:

> Bahrain obviously has the sovereign right to invited GCC forces into its territory under its defense and security agreements.... [The United States has] made clear that security alone cannot resolve the challenges facing Bahrain. As I said earlier this week, violence is not and cannot be the answer. A political process is. We have raised our concerns about the current measures directly with Bahraini officials and will continue to do so.

On April 30, 2011, according to the White House, President Obama spoke by phone to King Hamad and reportedly stated that Bahrain's stability depends on respect for the universal rights of the people of Bahrain, and a process of meaningful reform. At a May 5, 2011, House Foreign Affairs Committee hearing, State Department officials testified that the United States is "deeply concerned" by the "campaign of retribution" against the political opposition, adding that "security operations will not resolve the challenges Bahrain faces." President Obama's May 19, 2011, speech on the uprisings in the Middle East was critical of Bahrain, saying that the prospects for success of a dialogue with the opposition are compromised by the jailing of opposition figures. This U.S. position was restated in separate June 7, 2011, meetings between the Crown Prince andSecretary Clinton and President Obama. According to a White House statement, President Obama stressed to the Crown Prince that those

Bahraini forces or officials responsible for human rights abuses should be held "accountable."

The criticism continued in the course of the U.N. General Assembly meetings in New York in September 2011; in his September 21, 2011, speech to the body, President Obama said:

> In Bahrain, steps have been taken toward reform and accountability. We're pleased with that, but more is required. America is a close friend of Bahrain, and we will continue to call on the government and the main opposition bloc—the Wifaq—to pursue a meaningful dialogue that brings peaceful change that is responsive to the people. We believe the patriotism that binds Bahrainis together must be more powerful than the sectarian forces that would tear them apart. It will be hard, but it is possible.

The same day, the Ambassador-nominee to Bahrain, Thomas Krajeski, testified in confirmation hearings before the Senate Foreign Relations Committee. In his testimony, he reiterated Administration criticisms of the government response, saying the government "overreacted" to the unrest, as well as praise of its long record of reform and accommodation of some Shiite demands.

Critics of the U.S. position say that U.S. officials have not called for the Al Khalifa to step down and yield to a political transition, and there are no indications the Administration might take that position. As noted above, senior U.S. officials continue to meet with the Bahraini regime at high levels, although some observers say the United States advised King Hamad not to visit the United States in May 2011 to attend his son's college graduation. The U.S. position has been criticized by some as a U.S. "double standard," compared to the U.S. response to the 2011 unrest in Egypt, Tunisia, and Libya. The Administration did not send an official to testify at the May 13 Tom Lantos Human Rights Commission hearing discussed above. Some believe the government did not adequately protect a U.S. diplomat responsible in Manama responsible for human rights issues, Ludovic Hood. The State Department returned him to the United States in June 2011 because of perceived threats from Bahrainis who felt he was too critical of the government.

At the same time, the Administration has undertaken some efforts to help mediate in the crisis. Assistant Secretary of State for the Near East Jeffrey Feltman was sent to Bahrain in March 14, 2011, to attempt to achieve the beginning of a sustained dialogue between the government and theopposition. He visited again in mid-April. Outgoing Deputy Secretary of State James

Steinberg, along with Feltman and an NSC official, visited on May 17, 2011, meeting with senior Bahraini officials and again urging them to try to start dialogue with the opposition.

The Obama Administration, which presented its FY2012 budget request on February 14, 2011, just as the unrest in Bahrain was growing, has not announced any alteration of its military and anti-terrorism assistance or arms sales policy for Bahrain. Press reports say arms sales to Bahrain and other U.S. allies are under review because of the unrest in the region[11] although, as noted below, new sales to Bahrain were announced in September 2011. These sales have incurred strong objections from human rights activists, although the sales do not appear to include equipment that would be used against protesters. Levels of those sales and aid are discussed in the sections below.

Pre-2011 U.S. Posture on Bahraini Democracy and Human Rights

Well before the 2011 unrest began, successive U.S. Administrations have been accused by human rights groups and Bahraini Shiites of downplaying abuses against Bahrain's Shiite community. Critics point to Secretary of State Clinton's comments in Bahrain on December 3, 2010, referring to the October 2010 elections, saying: "I am impressed by the commitment that the government has to the democratic path that Bahrain is walking on. It takes time; we know that from our own experience."[12]

On the other hand, for many years prior to the 2011 unrest, the United States has sought to accelerate political reform in Bahrain and to empower its political societies through several programs. The primary vehicle has been the "Middle East Partnership Initiative (MEPI)," which began funding programs in Bahrain in 2003. MEPI funds have been used to help Bahrain build an independent judiciary, to strengthen the COR, to empower women, to conduct media training, and to promote legal reform. MEPI funds have also been used to fund AFL-CIO projects with Bahraini labor organizations, and to help Bahrain implement the U.S.-Bahrain FTA. In May 2006 Bahrain revoked the visa for the resident program director of the National Democratic Institute (NDI), and did not allow the office to reopen. NDI is conducting programs to enhance parliamentary capabilities through a local NGO. In February 2010, the MEPI office of State Department signed a memorandum of understanding with Bahrain to promote entrepreneurship there and promote opportunities for trade with U.S. small businesses. According to the State Department's International Religious Freedom report for July-December 2010 (September 13, 2011), "The U.S. government discusses religious freedom with the [Bahraini] government as part of its overall policy to promote human rights."

Other Human Rights Issues

Many of the general human rights issues are directly tied to the schism between the Sunni-led regime and the Shiite majority, as noted in U.S. government reports on human rights and religious freedom in Bahrain. Beyond that issue, State Department reports, such as the human rights report for 2010, note problems for non-Muslims and for opponents of the government. Bahrain allows freedom of worship for Christians, Jews, and Hindus although the constitution declares Islam the official religion. It should be noted that the State Department human rights report, released April 5, 2010, covers the period of calendar year 2010 and does not address the government response to the 2011 unrest.

There are several Bahraini human rights groups, mainly advocates for Shiite rights and causes. As noted above, two of the most prominent such groups are the Bahrain Human Rights Society and the Bahrain Transparency Society. Another is the Bahrain Center for Human Rights, founded by Abdul Hadi al-Khawaja, who is serving a life sentence for opposition activities.

Women's Rights

Bahrain has tended to be relatively progressive as far as law and regulations. However, as is the case with its neighbors, Bahrain's practices and customs tend to limit women's rights. Women can drive, own and inherit property, and initiate divorce cases, although religious courts may refuse a woman's divorce request. Some prominent women are campaigning for a codified family law that would enhance and secure women's rights, running into opposition from Bahraini clerics who are against granting more rights for women. The campaign for the law is backed by King Hamad's wife, Shaykha Sabeeka, and the Supreme Council for Women, which is the preeminent association that promotes women's rights in Bahrain.

To try to showcase its progressiveness, the government has promoted several women to high positions. The number of women in both chambers of the National Assembly are provided in Table 1, above. Since 2005, there have been two female ministers—Minister of Human Rights and Social Development Fatima bint Ahmad al-Balushi and Minister of Information and Culture Mai bint Muhammad Al Khalifa. A previous female minister of health, Nada Haffadh, resigned in October 2007 following allegations of corruption in her ministry by conservatives who oppose women occupying high-ranking positions. Two other women, including the president of the University of Bahrain, have ministerial rank. Ms. Huda Azar Nunu, an attorney and formerly the only Jew in the Shura Council, is ambassador to the United States.

Religious Freedom

On freedoms for religions other than Islam, the July-December 2011, State Department report on international religious freedom, in the section on Bahrain, says that respect for religious freedom exhibited "no change" since the prior report. Most of the report focuses on Sunni-Shiite differences, which are discussed as political issues above. According to the report, non-Muslims have been able to practice their religion privately without government interference, and to maintain places of worship. However, the government requires licenses for churches to operate, and has in the past threatened to shutter un-licensed churches serving Indian expatriates. The Baha'i faith, declared blasphemous in Iran and Afghanistan, has been discriminated against in Bahrain, although recent State Department human rights reports say that the Baha'i community now gathers and operates openly.

Labor Rights

On labor issues, Bahrain has been credited with significant labor reforms, including a 2002 law granting workers, including noncitizens, the right to form and join unions. The law holds that the right to strike is a legitimate means for workers to defend their rights and interests, but their right is restricted in practice, including a prohibition on strikes in the oil and gas, education, and health sectors. There are about 50 trade unions in Bahrain. The Shura Council has vetoed a proposed law that would have authorized formation of more than one union per company. All unions must join the General Federation of Bahrain Trade Unions (GFBTU).

Human Trafficking

On human trafficking, the State Department "Trafficking in Persons Report" for 2011, released June 27, 2011, keeps Bahrain's placement at Tier 2, on the grounds that it is investigating and prosecuting forced prosecution cases and convicted nine trafficking offenders during the reporting period. This is the same ranking Bahrain had following release of the 2010 Trafficking in Persons Report (June 14, 2010), when the "Watch List" designation was dropped. The 2009 report (June 16, 2009) assessed Bahrain as "Tier 2 - Watch List," with explanatory language similar to that of the 2008 report. That report had elevated Bahrain to Tier 2 Watch List, from the Tier 3 ranking (worst level) of the 2007 report.

Executions and Torture

Another issue that predated the 2011 unrest is that of executions. Human Rights Watch and other groups asserted that Bahrain is going against the international trend to end execution. InNovember 2009, Bahrain's Court of Cassation upheld the sentencing to death by firing squad of a citizen of Bangladesh. That sentenced was imposed for a 2005 murder. From 1977 until 2006, there were no executions in Bahrain.

Allegations of torture against Shiite opposition figures are widespread.[13] Witnesses at the May 13, 2011, hearing of the Tom Lantos Human Rights Commission asserted that torture was being used regularly on those arrested in the post-GCC intervention crackdown.

U.S.-BAHRAIN SECURITY AND FOREIGN POLICY RELATIONS[14]

U.S.-Bahrain relations are long-standing, intimate, and mutually reinforcing, raising the stakes for the United States in the unrest that has occurred there during 2011. A U.S. Embassy in Manama, Bahrain's capital, opened in September 1971 in conjunction with Bahrain's independence. At that time, the threat level in the Persian Gulf was perceived as relatively low. Since then, defense issues have become a central feature of U.S.-Bahrain relations. Although Iraq is no longer a strategic threat to the region because it cannot project power outside its borders, Iran's nuclear program is considered a growing threat to the Persian Gulf states, including Bahrain. There is also the issue of terrorism and piracy in the Gulf, as exemplified by a July 28, 2010, explosion on a Japanese oil tanker in that waterway. The explosion is widely suspected to have been a terrorist attack, and a faction linked to Al Qaeda (Abdullah Azzam Brigades) claimed responsibility.

In large part to keep powerful neighbors in check, Bahrain has long linked its security to the United States, and U.S. efforts to address threats in Iraq, Iran, and Afghanistan have benefitted from access to Bahraini facilities. In recognition of the relationship, in March 2002, President Bush (Presidential Determination 2002-10) designated Bahrain a "major non-NATO ally (MNNA)," a designation that facilitates U.S. arms sales.

U.S. Navy Headquarters in Bahrain

The cornerstone of U.S.-Bahrain defense relations is U.S. access to Bahrain's naval facilities. February 2008 marked the 60th anniversary of a U.S. naval command presence in Bahrain; MIDEASTFOR (U.S. Middle East Force), its successor, NAVCENT (naval component of U.S. Central Command), as well as the Fifth Fleet (reconstituted in June 1995) are headquartered there, at a sprawling facility called "Naval Support Activity-Bahrain." The facility now covers over 100 acres, and about 2,300 U.S. personnel, mostly Navy, are assigned there.[15] Some smaller U.S. ships (minesweepers) are docked there, but the Fifth Fleet also consists of a Carrier Battle Group, an Amphibious Ready Group, and various other ships that are afloat or which dock elsewhere in the region.

To further develop the naval facility (sometimes referred to as "Bahrain Island"), and other military facilities, the U.S. military is implementing a planned $580 million military construction program in Bahrain. Construction began in May 2010 to allow larger ships to dock at the naval facility; the project is expected to be completed, in several phases, by 2015. A January 2008 lease agreement between the United States and Bahrain allowed for the expansion by making available the decommissioned Mina (port) Salman. The bulk of the construction program is to expand the naval facility, but $45 million of the funds is to be used to expand an apron at Shaykh Isa Air Base and $19 million is to be used for a Special Operations Forces facility. Recent appropriations and requests to fund the construction include $54 million for FY2008 (Division 1 of P.L. 110- 161); no funds for FY2009; $41.5 million for FY2010 (P.L. 111-117); $258 million for FY2011 (Bahrain. P.L. 112-10); and $100 million requested for FY2012.

Some say that the United States should begin examining alternate facilities in the Gulf region in the expectation that continued Bahraini hosting of the U.S. naval headquarters has become unstable. On July 22, 2011, the U.S. Navy in Bahrain issued a statement refuting a British press report that the Navy is planning to relocate the facility. Should there be a decision to take that step, likely alternatives would include UAE or Qatar, although neither has expressed a position on whether it would be willing to host such an expanded facility.

Defense Pact and Cooperation with U.S. Operations in Iraq and Afghanistan

Bahrain was part of the U.S.-led allied coalition that ousted Iraq from Kuwait in 1991, hosting 17,500 troops and 250 combat aircraft at Shaykh Isa Air Base (mentioned above). Expanding on the agreement under which Bahrain hosted U.S. naval headquarters, Bahrain and the UnitedStates signed a 10-year defense pact signed on October 28, 1991, seven months after the ousting of Iraqi troops from Kuwait. The pact was renewed in October 2001, and was presumably to be up for renewal in October 2011. However, press and expert accounts in August 2011 indicate that, a few months after the September 11, 2001, attacks on the United States, the Bush Administration may have extended the pact a further five years, to 2016. The U.S. Defense Department has not publicly confirmed these stories, although one U.S. official, on background, said the pact was previously extended beyond October 2011.[16] The pact not only provides the United States access to Bahrain's air bases and to pre-position strategic materiel (mostly U.S. Air Force munitions), but also requires consultations with Bahrain if its security is threatened, and it expanded exercises and U.S. training of Bahraini forces.[17]

Following the liberation of Kuwait in February 1991, there were about 1,300 U.S. military personnel in Bahrain during the 1990s to contain Saddam Hussein's Iraq, and Bahraini pilots flew strikes over Iraq during the war; Iraq fired nine Scud missiles at Bahrain during the war, of which three hit facilities there. Bahrain hosted the regional headquarters for U.N. weapons inspections in Iraq during 1991-1998, and the U.S.-led Multinational Interdiction Force (MIF) that enforced a U.N. embargo on Iraq during 1991-2003. Since the early 1990s, the United States has reportedly stationed two Patriot anti-missile batteries there.[18]

Post-September 11 and Post-Saddam Cooperation

The naval headquarters, the U.S. use of which predated the defense pact, has been used to coordinate the operations of over 20 U.S. warships performing support missions for U.S. and allied naval operations related to the U.S. military operations ongoing in Iraq and Afghanistan. These ships are also part of Combined Task Force (CTF) 151 and 152 that seek to interdict the movement of terrorists, arms, or weapons of mass destruction (WMD)-related technology and narcotics across the Arabian Sea. These task forces also seek to counter piracy in the Arabia Sea. In March 2008, Bahrain took a turn in a rotation to command CTF-152, and it commanded again in December 2010.

Bahrain commanded an anti-piracy task force in Gulf/Arabian Sea waters in October 2010. These operations are offshoots of Operation Enduring Freedom (OEF) in Afghanistan, which ousted the Taliban after the September 11 attacks. Bahrain allowed the United States to fly combat missions from its bases (Shaykh Isa Air Base) in both OEF and the war to oust Saddam Hussein in March-April 2003 (Operation Iraqi Freedom, OIF). During both OEF and OIF, Bahrain publicly deployed its U.S.-supplied frigate warship (the *Subha*) to help protect U.S. ships, and it sent ground and air assets to Kuwait in support of OIF. Bahrain hosted about 4,000 U.S. military personnel during major combat of OEF (October 2001-May 2003).

Bahrain and UAE have been the only Gulf states to deploy their own forces to provide aid to Afghanistan. In January 2009, Bahrain sent 100 police officers to Afghanistan on a two-year tour to help U.S./NATO-led stabilization operations there.

Bahrain's participation in OIF came despite domestic opposition in Bahrain to that war. Because of its limited income, Bahrain has not contributed funds to Iraq reconstruction, but it attended the "Expanded Neighbors of Iraq" regional conference process which last met in Kuwait on April 22, 2008. That process was suspended in late 2008 as Iraq stabilized and the United States has begun the process of withdrawal, expected to be complete by the end of 2011. On October 16, 2008, Bahrain's first post-Saddam ambassador to Iraq (Saleh Ali al-Maliki) presented his credentials in Baghdad, in line with King Hamad's pledge to President Bush in March 2008. Some of the other Gulf states, most notably Saudi Arabia, have still not established a full embassy in Iraq, in part due to differences between Saudi Arabia and the Shiite-led government of Prime Minister Nuri al-Maliki.

U.S. Arms Transfers and Military Aid

To assist Bahrain's ability to cooperate with the United States on regional security issues, Congress and successive Administrations, citing Bahrain's limited income, have supported military assistance to Bahrain's small force. The main recipient of such assistance is the relatively small Bahrain Defense Force (BDF), which has about 13,000 personnel (plus about 1,200 National Guard). The BDF and the police are run by Sunni Bahrainis, but are said to supplement their ranks with unknown percentages of paid Sunni Muslim recruits from neighboring countries, including Pakistan, Yemen, Jordan, Iraq, and elsewhere. Until 1998, Bahrain's internal security services were run by a former British colonial police officer, Ian Henderson, who had a reputation among Shiites for using repressive measures. The current director of the internal security service is Shaykh Khalifa bin Abdullah Al Khalifa, considered a hardliner in the royal family.

Bahrain is eligible to receive grant "excess defense articles" (EDA). The United States transferred the FFG-7 "Perry class" frigate *Subha* (see above) as EDA in July 1997. According to the State Department's FY2012 budget request, the U.S. Navy is supporting providing another frigate (an "extended deck frigate") to Bahrain as EDA because the *Subha* is approaching the end of its service life. In 1996, the United States gave Bahrain a no-cost five-year lease on 60 M60A3 tanks; title subsequently passed to Bahrain. Foreign Military Financing (FMF) was suspended for Bahrain in FY1994 but restarted in appreciation of Bahrain's support in OEF and OIF.

Recent FMF (and funds provided under "Section 1206" of the National Defense Authorization Act of 2006, P.L. 109-163), have been provided to help Bahrain maintain U.S.-origin weapons, to enhance inter-operability with U.S. forces, to augment Bahrain's air defenses, to support and upgrade the avionics of its F-16 fleet, and to improve counter-terrorism capabilities. As an example, the United States has supplied Bahrain with a coastal radar system that reportedly provides Bahrain and the U.S. Navy a 360-degree field of vision around Bahrain.[19] Some funds have been used to build up Bahrain's Special Operations forces. The Defense Department estimates that, in part due to U.S. assistance, as of FY2008, about 45% of Bahrain's forces are fully capable of integrating into a U.S.-led coalition.

As noted in *Table 3*, small amounts of International Military Education and Training funds (IMET) are provided to Bahrain to inculcate principles of civilian control of the military, democracy, and interoperability with U.S. forces. During FY2010, 26 Bahraini students attended U.S. military schools.

Purchases with National Funds

Despite its limited funds (Bahrain's total government budget was about $6 billion in 2009), Bahrain has purchased some U.S. systems. In 1998, Bahrain purchased 10 U.S.-made F-16Cs from new production, worth about $390 million. In 1999, the United States sold Bahrain 26 Advanced Medium-Range Air-to-Air Missiles (AMRAAM) to arm the F-16s, although some Members were concerned that the AMRAAM sale could promote an arms race in the Gulf. Section 581 of the FY1990 foreign operations appropriation act (P.L. 101-167) made Bahrain the only Gulf state eligible to receive the STINGER shoulder-fired anti-aircraft missile, and the United States has sold Bahrain about 70 Stingers since 1990. (This authorization has been repeated in subsequent legislation.) To allay congressional concerns about possible U.S. promotion of missile proliferation in the region, an August 2000 sale of 30 Army Tactical Missile Systems (ATACMs, a system of short-range ballistic missiles fired from a multiple rocket launcher) included an agreement for joint U.S.-Bahraini control of the weapon. (A notification of a possible sale to Bahrain of 30 ATACM missiles and associated equipment, valued at about $70 million, was sent to Congress on November 4, 2010. Lockheed Martin is the prime contractor for the missiles.)

Among recent sales notified to Congress by the Defense Security Cooperation Agency (DSCA) are: 180 "Javelin" anti-armor missiles and 60 launch units, worth up to $42 million; nine UH- 60M Blackhawk helicopters worth up to $252 million; six Bell search and recovery helicopters, valued at about $160 million, notified August 3, 2007; up to 25 AMRAAMs (Raytheon Missile Systems Corp.) and associated equipment, valued at about $74 million, notified on July 28, 2009.

September 2011 Humvee and TOW Sale. One sale, notified on September 14, 2011, is increasingly controversial because it was announced seven months after the unrest began, and has been agreed to despite U.S. criticism of Bahrain's crackdown. It is for a proposed sale of 44 "Humvee" armored vehicles and several hundred TOW missiles (of which 50 are to be "bunker busters"), along with associated equipment and support, worth an estimated $53 million. Although not considered large in dollar terms, or of particularly sophisticated equipment, the sale has incurred opposition from several human rights groups who assert that the sale represents U.S. downplaying of the abuses committed by the Bahraini government in the course of the unrest. Human rights groups and Bahraini opposition figures say the regime could use the Humvees, in particular, in their efforts to crack down on protests. State Department officials said the sale would not violate the intent of the "Leahy amendment"—a provision of foreign aid and defense appropriations laws that forbids U.S. sales of equipment to security units that have committed human rights abuses.[20] The notification came several months after U.S. arms sales policy to Gulf allies and other Middle Eastern countries was reportedly placed under review in light of regional unrest that began in early 2011, including in Bahrain. Two joint resolutions have been introduced in the 112th Congress to block the sale: S.J.Res. 28, introduced by Sen. Ron Wyden, and H.J.Res. 80, introduced by Rep. James McGovern. Both joint resolutions would prohibit the sale unless the Administration certifies that Bahrain is rectifying the alleged abuses connected to its suppression of the uprising in 2011. To block a proposed arms sale would require passage of a joint resolution to do so, and with a veto-proof majority, because President Obama could veto a joint resolution of disapproval in order to complete the sale.

Some of the most recent sales are in accordance with the State Department's "Gulf Security Dialogue," begun in 2006 to counter Iran, and under which a total of about $20 billion worth of U.S. weapons might be sold to the Gulf monarchy states. Only a small portion of that total sales volume is reportedly slated for Bahrain.

Anti-Terrorism Cooperation

Bahrain's cooperation in post-September 11 regional security operations was discussed above. As far as terrorists operating inside Bahrain itself, the State Department's report on international terrorism for 2010 (released August 18, 2011) again credits Bahrain for having "worked to actively counter terrorist finance," as well as for enhanced border control capabilities, for a realignment of institutional responsibilities that resulted in greater capacity and interagency cooperation, and for successfully prosecuting a number of cases under its 2006 counterterrorism law. The report for 2010 dropped the criticism of the previous year's report that Bahrain had not overcome legal constraints that have sometimes hampered its ability to detain and prosecute suspected terrorists.

Bahrain also continues to host the Middle East and North Africa Financial Action Task Force (MENA/FATF) secretariat and its Central Bank, Financial Information Unit (within the Central Bank), and local banks cooperate with U.S. efforts against terrorism financing and money laundering. As noted by the State Department in the FY2012 budget justification, some of the U.S. assistance to Bahrain (NADR funds) are used to provide training to its counter-terrorism institutions and to augment the ability of Bahraini forces to protect U.S. diplomatic and military facilities in Bahrain. The Bahraini Ministry of Interior is the lead agency that receives this support and, according to the FY2012 budget justification, the Administration is "reviewing" the use of this aid to ensure that none was used "against protestors" in the 2011 unrest.

Relations with and Cooperation Against Iran

As noted previously, Bahrain focuses its foreign policy intently on Iran, which has purportedly demonstrated an ability to influence Bahrain's domestic security to a greater degree than has any other regional power. Bahrain perceives Iran as willing and able to support Shiite groups against Bahrain's Sunni-dominated government. In December 1981, and then again in June 1996—a time when Iran was actively seeking to export its Islamic revolution—Bahrain publicly accused Iran of trying to organize a coup by pro-Iranian Bahraini Shiites (the Islamic Front for the Liberation of Bahrain, IFLB).

The issue of alleged Iranian involvement in the 2011 unrest has risen to the surface of the debate in Bahrain and the United States. Ambassador Krajeski (see above) testified on September 21 that the United States "saw no evidence of Iranian instigation" of the unrest, but that the United States is concerned "about Iranian exploitation" of it. U.S. officials reportedly believe that Iran has urged hardline Bahraini Shiite factions not to compromise.[21] On April 14, 2011, U.S. officials, speaking on background, told journalists that Tehran is debating how much aid, if any, to provide to Bahrain's opposition, and that there was some information to indicate that Iran might have transferred small amounts of weapons to Bahraini oppositionists.[22]

Bahraini leaders have issued far stronger allegations. On March 21, 2011, King Hamad indirectly accused Iran of involvement in the unrest by saying a "foreign plot" had been foiled by the GCC assistance and on April 17, 2011, the Bahraini government sent a letter to U.N. Secretary-General Ban Ki Moon formally alleging that the pro-Iranian Shiite faction Hezbollah is seeking to destabilize Bahrain with "logistical help" from unnamed countries (but clearly referring to Iran). The two countries withdrew their ambassadors in mid-March 2011. In an event that gave the Bahraini government some justification for its criticism, on May 16, 2011, Iranian warships began an effort to transport 150 pro-Bahrain opposition Iranian Shiites to Bahrain, but turned back the following day for fear of provoking a clash with GCC ships. This event came two days after Iran's Foreign Minister praised a speech by King Hamad that appeared intended to lower tensions with Iran by "offering friendship" to Tehran. The foreign ministers of the two countries held talks on September 27, 2011, at the sidelines of the U.N. General Assembly meetings in New York.

Well before the 2011 unrest, Bahrain's fears about Iran had been infused by lingering suspicions, sometimes fed by Iranian actions, that Iran never accepted the results of the 1970 U.N. survey giving Bahrain independence rather than integration with Iran. Those findings were endorsed by U.N. Security Council Resolution 278, which was ratified by Iran's parliament. After these official determinations, Bahrain had considered the issue closed, after over a century of Persian contestation of Bahraini sovereignty. Those contests included an effort by Reza Shah Pahlavi of Iran in the 1930s to deny Bahrain the right to grant oil concessions to the United States and Britain.

In recent years, Bahrain's leadership—and other countries in the region— have reacted strongly against statements by Iranian editorialists and advisers to Iranian leaders appearing to reassert Iran's claim. One such example was a July 2007 Iranian newspaper article reasserting the Iranian claim to Bahrain. However, that article, along with the Bahraini Crown Prince's November 3, 2007, comment that Iran is developing a nuclear weapon (Iran claims it is developing only civilian nuclear power), did not mar the visit of Iranian President Ahmadinejad on November 17, 2007. In March 2009 by former Iranian parliament speaker Ali Akbar Nateq Nuri, now an advisor to Iran's Supreme Leader, again referring to Bahrain as Iran's 14th province. Iran's ForeignMinistry immediately tried to limit any diplomatic damage by asserting respect for Bahrain'ssovereignty and independence, but some Arab governments sharply criticized the Nateq Nuri comments. Morocco broke relations with Iran as a response.

In connection with its own concerns about Iran, Bahrain has supported the U.S. position that Iran is not fully cooperating with U.N. Security Council requirements to verifiably demonstrate that its nuclear program is not a cover for a nuclear weapons program. In the joint news conference with Secretary Clinton on December 3, 2010, referenced earlier, the foreign minister restated Bahrain's support for Iran's right to nuclear power for peaceful uses. However, it stated forthright that "when it comes to taking that [nuclear] power, to developing it into a cycle for weapon grade, that is something that we can never accept, and we can never live with in this region."[23]

At the same time, so as not to provide Iran a pretext to pressure Bahrain, Bahrain's leaders have sometimes tried to silence voices in Bahrain that publicly attack Iran. An example is the one-day suspension in 2009 of the newspaper *Akhbar al Khaleej (Gulf News)* for running an editorial by a Bahrain Shura Council member who criticized Iranian leaders. Bahrain regularly supports the invitation of high-ranking Iranian officials to the annual International Institute for Security Studies (IISS) conference in Bahrain called the "Manama Dialogue," held every December. At times, there have been expectations that U.S. officials might meet with Iranian officials at the margins of the conference, although such meetings have not taken place in practice. Iranian officials have sometimes been known to cancel their travel to the meeting on short notice, particularly if they sense that the conference will feature U.S. or other criticism of Iran.

Bahrain-Iran Gas Development Deal and Other Economic Ties

Another way in which Bahrain stays engaged with Iran is through discussions of major energy projects with Iran and by conducting normal trade and banking ties with it. The 2007Ahmadinejad visit resulted in a preliminary agreement for Bahrain to buy 1.2 billion cubic feet per day (for 25 years) of Iranian gas via an undersea pipeline to be built. The deal would have involved a $4 billion investment by Bahrain to develop Phases 15 and 16 of Iran's South Pars gas field, which presumably would be the source of the gas that Bahrain would import. The March 2009 comments of Nateq Nuri, discussed above, led to the suspension of this deal. On October 21, 2009, Bahrain's Minister of Oil and Gas Abd al-Husayn Mirza said talks on the deal would "resume soon." There is a widespread assumption that the 2011 unrest has clouded the prospects for the deal, but Bahraini officials said in June 2011 that it has not been cancelled outright.

There are no indications that Iran-Bahrain commerce has been affected by the 2011 unrest. Energy market observers say that Bahrain energy firms are still supplying gasoline to Iran. No U.N. Security Council Resolution bars such sales, but a U.S. law signed on July 1, 2010—the Comprehensive Iran Sanctions, Accountability, and Divestment Act of 2010 (CISADA, P.L. 111-195)—provides for sanctions against foreign firms that sell more than $1 million worth of gasoline to Iran. Some energy firms in the Gulf, including in Kuwait, reportedly have become reticent to continue supplying gasoline to Iran because of the U.S. action, but Bahrain is not known to have publicly disavowed further gasoline sales to Iran.[24]

In March 2008, the U.S. Department of Justice sanctioned Future Bank, headquartered in Bahrain, because it is controlled and partially owned by Iran's Bank Melli. The sanctions, under Executive Order 13382 (anti-proliferation), prevent U.S. citizens from participating in transactions with Future Bank and require the freezing of any U.S.-based bank assets. The Bank remains in operation.

Other Foreign Policy Issues

Bahrain has close relations with the other GCC states, in particular Saudi Arabia, as evidenced by its turn to Saudi Arabia to help it deal with the 2011 unrest. Virtually all the GCC states have political structures similar to that of Bahrain, and several have substantial Shiite minorities (although not majorities, as Bahrain does). Saudi Arabia's Shiites (about 10% of the population) are located mostly in the eastern provinces, across a causeway constructed in 1986 that connects the two countries. This linkage partly explains Saudi concerns about the unrest shaking the royal family in Bahrain. Because of historic property and other ties between their two royal families Kuwait was briefly touted as a potential mediator in the Bahraini political crisis. Kuwaiti Shiites in Kuwait's parliament have argued against Kuwait's siding firmly with the Al Khalifa regime. However, the Kuwaiti government has, as noted, at least symbolically joined the GCC military deployments to Bahrain on the side of the government. Kuwait's Prime Minister visited Bahrain on July 5, 2011.

On other regional issues, unlike Qatar and UAE, Bahrain did not play a significant role in assisting the Libyan opposition to the rule of Colonel Muammar Al Qadhafi. Bahrain's intervention in Libya could have been viewed as a contradiction – supporting a revolutionary movement in another Arab state while arguing that its domestic opposition's grievances lacked legitimacy and that the opposition was beholden to Iran. In August 2011, Bahrain joined Saudi Arabia and Kuwait in withdrawing its Ambassador to Syria, probably because Syria is Iran's main Middle Eastern ally and Bahrain wanted to signal retaliation for what it claims is Iranian intervention in Bahrain's internal affairs.

Qatar Territorial Disputes[25]

The United States cooperates closely with both Qatar and Bahrain, which is why the Bahrain- Qatar territorial dispute was closely watched by U.S. policymakers. The resolution of the dispute has partly removed these tensions as an issue for U.S. Gulf policy. Qatar, like Bahrain, is a GCC monarchy; however, their relations have been sometimes acrimonious because of territorial disputes with roots in the 18th century, when the ruling families of both countries controlled parts of the Arabian peninsula. Qatar-Bahrain relations have improved since an International Court of Justice ruled on March 16, 2001, on the disputes. The ICJ ruled in favor of Qatar on some of the issues, and in favor of Bahrain on others, but the central dispute—over the

Hawar Islands—was decided in favor of Bahrain. Qatar expressed disappointment over the ruling but said it accepted it as binding, and the two have since muted mutual criticism and cooperated on major regional issues. The territorial disputes were referred to the ICJ by Qatar in 1991 after clashes in 1986 in which Qatar landed military personnel on a man-made reef (Fasht al-Dibal) that was in dispute, and took some Bahrainis prisoner. Saudi mediation in the 1986-1991 period proved fruitless. That reef was awarded to Qatar in the ICJ ruling. However, the ICJ ruled against Bahrain's claim to the town of Zubara on the Qatari mainland, where some members of the Al Khalifa family were long buried. Two smaller islands, Janan and Hadd Janan, were ruled not part of the Hawar Islands group and were awarded to Qatar.

Arab-Israeli Issues

On the Arab-Israeli dispute, Bahrain has not been as significant a mediator or broker as have its larger neighbors in the Gulf or broader Middle East. Bahrain has not taken a leading role in recent efforts to reconcile Hamas and Fatah to rebuild Palestinian unity, for example. On the other hand, Bahrain is not inactive on the issue: On July 16, 2009, Crown Prince Salman authored an op-edcalling on the Arab states to do more to communicate directly with the Israeli people on their ideas for peaceful resolution of the dispute.[26] Following on that idea, on October 1, 2009, the foreign minister called for direct talks with Israel. In the previously cited December 3, 2010, joint press conference with the foreign minister, Secretary of State Clinton expressed appreciation for Bahrain's support of Palestinian Authority leaders who are trying to build viable institutions and rule of law in the Palestinian territories. However, like most Arab states, Bahrain is supporting the efforts of Palestinian Authority President Mahmoud Abbas to obtain U.N. recognition for a State of Palestine, despite U.S. opposition to granting such recognition without an overall Palestinian peace settlement with Israel.

Earlier, Bahrain participated in the 1990-1996 multilateral Arab-Israeli talks, and it hosted a session on the environment (October 1994). Bahrain did not follow Oman and Qatar in exchanging trade offices with Israel. In September 1994, all GCC states ceased enforcing secondary and tertiary boycotts of Israel while retaining the ban on direct trade (primary boycott). In conjunction with the U.S.-Bahrain FTA, Bahrain dropped the primary boycott and closed boycott-related offices in Bahrain.

Still, the Arab-Israeli dispute always has the potential to become a political issue within Bahrain. Islamist hard-liners in Bahrain have accused the government of trying to "normalize" relations with Israel, citing the government's sending a delegate to the November 27, 2007, summit on Middle East peace in Annapolis, the foreign minister's meeting with Israeli officials at U.N. meetings in September 2007, and its October 2009 proposal of a "regional organization" that would group Iran, Turkey, Israel, and the Arab states. That proposal has not been implemented to date. In late October 2009, the elected COR passed a bill making it a crime (punishable by up to five years in jail) for Bahrainis to travel to Israel or hold talks with Israelis. The bill, which has not proceeded to become law (concurrence by the upper house, and acceptance by the King), apparently was a reaction to a visit by Bahraini officials to Israel in July 2009. The visit was to obtain the release of five Bahrainis taken prisoner by Israel when it seized a ship bound with goods for Gaza, which is controlled by Hamas. In June 2010, Sunni and Shiite Islamists in Bahrain held a demonstration to denounced the Israeli seizure of a ship in a flotilla intended to run the Israeli blockade of the Hamas-run Gaza Strip.

ECONOMIC ISSUES

Like the other Gulf states, Bahrain was affected by the international financial crisis of 2008-2009, but perhaps to a lesser extent than the wealthier states of Kuwait, UAE, and Saudi Arabia. Bahrain did not experience the construction and real estate "bubble" to the degree that this occurred in, for example, UAE. It is also apparently being affected by the 2011 unrest; in May 2011 Moody's, a bond rating agency, downgraded the quality of Bahrain's bonds, thereby costing the government more to borrow funds. Bahrain had been hoping the unrest would not force cancellation of a high-profile, funds-generating Formula One auto race in October 2011, but race organizers decided not to hold the event from Bahrain.

Bahrain has little cushion to deal with economic downturns. It has the lowest oil and gas reserves of the Gulf monarchy states, estimated respectively at 210 million barrels of oil and 5.3 trillion cubic feet of gas. Some economic statistics are presented in Table 2. Without the ample oil or gas resources of its neighbors, Bahrain has diversified its economy by emphasizing banking and financial services (about 25.5% of GDP). At current rates of production (35,000 barrels per day of crude oil), Bahrain's onshore oil reserves will be exhausted in 15 years, but Saudi Arabia shares equally with Bahrain the 300,000 barrels per day produced from the offshore Abu Safa field. The United States buys virtually no oil from Bahrain; the major U.S. import from it is aluminum. Aluminum and other manufacturing sectors in Bahrain account for the existence in Bahrain of a vibrant middle and working class among its citizens. However, these classes are largely composed of Shiites, and this has made many Shiites envious of the "ownership class" of Sunni Muslims. On the other hand, many Shiites own businesses and have done well economically.

To encourage reform and signal U.S. appreciation, the United States and Bahrain signed an FTA on September 14, 2004. Implementing legislation was signed January 11, 2006 (P.L. 109-169). However, in light of the unrest, the AFL-CIO has urged the United States to void the FTA on the grounds that Bahrain is preventing free association of workers and abridging their rights.

In 2010, the United States exported $1.25 billion worth of goods to Bahrain, and imported $420 million in goods from that country. In 2005, total bilateral trade was about $780 million, suggesting that trade has expanded significantly following the FTA.

Table 2. Some Basic Facts About Bahrain

Population	About 740,000, of which 503,000 are citizens
Religions	81% Muslim, 9% Christian, 10% other
GDP (purchasing power parity)	$28 billion (2009)
Budget	$5.81 billion revenues, $5.86 billion expenditures (2009)
External Debt	$11 billion (2009)
Inflation Rate	3% (2009)
GDP Real Growth Rate	2.9% in 2009, down from over 6% in 2008
Size of Bahrain Defense Forces (BDF)	About 13,000, plus about 1,200 National Guard. Some personne are expatriates, including other Arab and Pakistani.

Source: CIA, *The World Factbook.*

Table 3. U.S. Assistance to Bahrain ($ in millions)

	FY 03	FY 04	FY 05	FY 06	FY 07	FY 08	FY 09	FY 2010	FY 2011	FY 2012 request
FMF	90.0	24.6	18.847	15.593	14.998	3.968	8.0	19.0	15.46	25.0
IMET	0.448	0.600	0.649	0.651	0.616	0.622	.661	.670	.700	.700
NADR			1.489	2.761	.776	0.744	.500	1.10	1.5	.500
"Section 1206"				5.3	24.54	4.3	16.2			

Notes: IMET = International Military Education and Training Funds, used mainly to enhance BDF military professionalism and promote U.S. values. NADR = Non-Proliferation, Anti-Terrorism, De-Mining and Related Programs, used to sustain Bahrain's counterterrorism capabilities and interdict terrorists. Section 1206 are DOD funds used to train and equip Bahrain's special forces, its coastal surveillance and patrol capabilities, and to develop its counter terrorism assessment capabilities. (Named for a section of the FY2006 Defense Authorization Act, P.L. 109-163.) FY2008 funds derived from FY2008 supplemental (P.L. 110-252), and the Consolidated appropriation (P.L. 110-329). FY2009 funds included funding from FY2008 supplemental (P.L. 110-252) as well as regular appropriation (P.L. 111-8). FY2010 funds are from Consolidated Appropriation (P.L. 111-117). FY2011 funds are appropriated by P.L. 112-10, Continuing Appropriations for FY2011.

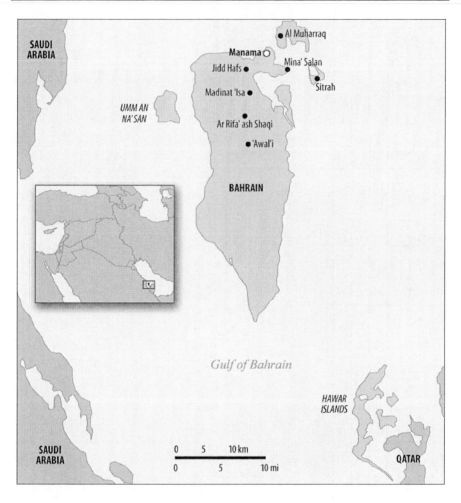

Figure 1. Bahrain.

End Notes

[1] Much of the information in this section is from State Department reports: 2010 Country Reports on Human Rights Practices (April 8, 2011); the International Religious Freedom Report for July – December 2010 (September 13, 2011); and the Trafficking in Persons Report for 2011 (June 27, 2011). CRS has no means to independently investigate the human rights situation in Bahrain or confirm allegations of specific human rights abuses there.

[2] Government officials dispute that the Shiite community is as large a majority as the 70% figure used in most factbooks and academic work on Bahrain. The Shiite community in Bahrain consists of the more numerous "Baharna," who are of Arab ethnicity and descended from Arab tribes who inhabited the area from pre-Islamic times. Shiites of Persian ethnicity are

less numerous, and arrived in Bahrain over the past 400 years. They speak Persian and generally do not integrate with the Baharna or with Sunni Arabs.

[3] The name of this official is similar to that of the Foreign Minister, Khalid bin Ahmad bin Mohammad Al Khalifa.

[4] "Bahrain Hard-Liners Call for Royal Family to Go." Cable News Network website, March 9, 2011.

[5] Some accounts differ on the involvement of the Peninsula Shield force, with some observers arguing that members of the force have participated directly in suppressing protests, and others accepting the Bahrain/GCC view that the GCC force is only guarding key locations and infrastructure.

[6] Erika Solomon. "Bahrain Sentences 8 Activists to Life Terms." Washington Post, June 23, 2011.

[7] Mohamed Hasni. "Bahrain Opens Dialogue Buoyed by Shiite Attendance." Agence France Presse, July 2, 2011.

[8] Author conversations with representatives of and observers close to the regime. April 2011.

[9] Secretary of State Clinton Comments on the Situation in the Middle East. http://www. youtube. com/watch?v= GbucMZUg3Gc.

[10] "Obama Welcomes Bahrain Cabinet Reshuffle." Reuters, February 27, 2011.

[11] Adam Entous. "U.S. Reviews Arms Sales Amid Turmoil." *Wall Street Journal*, February 23, 2011.

[12] Department of State. "Remarks With Foreign Minister Al Khalifa After Their Meeting." December 3, 2010.

[13] Human Rights Watch. "Bahrain: Torture Redux." February 2010.

[14] Information in this section obtained from a variety of press reports, and the Defense Security Cooperation Agency (DSCA).

[15] Unclassified information provided to CRS by the Department of Defense. Figures are as of June 30, 2010.

[16] "U.S.-Bahrain Defense Pact Renewed." Agence France Presse, August 5, 2011.

[17] Details of the U.S.-Bahrain defense agreement are classified. Some provisions are discussed in Sami Hajjar, *U.S. Military Presence in the Gulf: Challenges and Prospects* (U.S. Army War College: Strategic Studies Institute), March 2002, p. 27.

[18] Walter Pincus. "Bahrain Government's Ties With the United States Run Deep." *Washington Post*, February 22, 2011.

[19] "Bahrain Government's Ties With the United States Run Deep." Op. cit.

[20] James Lobe. "Bahrain: U.S. Congress Urged to Reject Arms Sales." IPS News Service, September 29, 2011.

[21] http://www.stripes.com/gates-protracted-bahrain-negotiations-allowing-greater-iran-influence-1.137532.

[22] Adam Entous and Matthew Rosenberg. "U.S. Says Iran Helps Crackdown in Syria." *Wall Street Journal,* April 14, 2011.

[23] Department of State. Transcript of Remarks by Secretary Clinton and Foreign Minister Al Khalifa. December 3, 2010.

[24] CRS conversations with foreign diplomats, including some from the Gulf. July–September 2010.

[25] See The Estimate. Dossier: The Bahrain-Qatar Border Dispute: The World Court Decision, Part 1 and Part 2. March 23, 2001, and April 6, 2001.

[26] "Arabs Need to Talk to the Israelis." *The Washington Post*. July 16, 2009.

In: Bahrain and Jordan   ISBN: 978-1-61942-605-4
Editors: K. Buck and T. J. McPherson   © 2012 Nova Science Publishers, Inc.

Chapter 2

JORDAN: BACKGROUND AND U.S. RELATIONS[*]

Jeremy M. Sharp

SUMMARY

This report provides an overview of Jordanian politics and current issues in U.S.-Jordanian relations. It provides a brief discussion of Jordan's government and economy and of its cooperation in promoting Arab-Israeli peace and other U.S. policy objectives in the Middle East.

Several issues in U.S.-Jordanian relations are likely to figure in decisions by Congress and the Administration on future aid to and cooperation with Jordan. These include the stability of the Jordanian regime, the role of Jordan in the Arab-Israeli peace process, the possibility of U.S.- Jordanian nuclear energy cooperation, and U.S.-Jordanian military and intelligence cooperation.

Although the United States and Jordan have never been linked by a formal treaty, they have cooperated on a number of regional and international issues over the years. The country's small size and lack of major economic resources have made it dependent on aid from Western andfriendly Arab sources. U.S. support, in particular, has helped Jordan address serious vulnerabilities, both internal and external. Jordan's geographic position, wedged between Israel, Syria, Iraq, and Saudi Arabia, has made it vulnerable to the strategic designs of

---

[*] This is an edited, reformatted and augmented version of Congressional Research Service Report RL33546, dated June 21, 2011.

its more powerful neighbors, but has also given Jordan an important role as a buffer between these potential adversaries. In 1990, Jordan's unwillingness to join the allied coalition against Iraq disrupted its relations with the United States and the Persian Gulf states; however, relations improved throughout the 1990s as Jordan played an increasing role in the Arab-Israeli peace process and distanced itself from Saddam Hussein's Iraq.

The United States has provided economic and military aid, respectively, to Jordan since 1951 and 1957. Total U.S. aid to Jordan through FY2011 amounted to approximately $12.47 billion. Levels of aid have fluctuated, increasing in response to threats faced by Jordan and decreasing during periods of political differences or worldwide curbs on aid funding. On September 22, 2008, the U.S. and Jordanian governments reached an agreement whereby the United States agreed to provide a total of $660 million in annual foreign assistance to Jordan over a five-year period. For FY2012, the Administration is requesting $663.7 million for Jordan in total military and economic aid.

RECENT DEVELOPMENTS

- **King Abdullah Proposes New Reforms.** In a nationally televised speech on June 12, 2011, King Abdullah II proposed that in the future, parliamentary majorities would be able to form governments rather than the king himself.[1] He offered no specific timetable for this change, but suggested that the process of reform could take between two to three years. Some opposition groups and figures asserted that the king had previously discussed similar proposals and that this latest proposal lacks detail.

- **Protests in Tafila, King's Convoy Attacked?** According to various media reports, both during and after a recent visit to the town of Tafila (109 miles south of Amman), a crowd of young rioters clashed with local police and reportedly threw stones at the king's motorcade. Soon thereafter, there were reports that the Amman office of *Agence France Presse*, the news agency that initially broke the story of possible violence against the king's convoy, was raided and vandalized. King Abdullah II recently announced the creation of a Tafila Development Fund, valued at $21 million, to create jobs for residents, among other development projects.

- **King Abdullah II Interview on Peace Process** In a recent interview with the *Washington Post*, King Abdullah II stated that "2011 will be, I think, a very bad year for peace." He added that "Although we will continue to try to bring both sides to the table, I am the most pessimistic I have been in 11 years.... If it's not atwo-state solution, then it's a one-state solution.... And then, is it going to beapartheid, or is it going to be democracy?"[2]

- **National Dialogue Committee Recommendations.** In June 2011, the National Dialogue Committee recommended that the size of parliament be increased from 120 to 130 seats and that future elections be overseen by an independent panel of judges rather than the Interior Ministry.[3] The committee also proposed that the government should ease requirements for the formation of political parties by lowering the number of people required to found a party from 500 to 250, of whom at least 25 would have to be women.[4] The committee also recommended that the electoral system be altered to designate seats both at the governorate level (115 total) and the national level (15).[5] Islamists in the opposition havecriticized the proposed electoral law changes, claiming that 15 seats allotted for a national list is insufficient, and that voting patterns along tribal and familial lines will continue to the benefit of the monarchy and its allies.

- **Saudi Arabia and the Gulf Cooperation Council Aid Jordan.** In June 2011, Saudi Arabia provided Jordan with a $400 million cash grant in order to stabilize Jordan's finances. A month earlier, the Gulf Cooperation Council (GCC) welcomed Jordan to apply for membership to the regional organization which, if approved, could further boost the kingdom's finances at a time when it is facing significant budget deficits. The GCC twice rejected Jordan's application for GCC membership—once in the 1980s, and once in 1996.

- **Ministers Resign in Fallout from Corruption Scandal.** In May 2011, the ministers of justice and health resigned after news broke that a convicted businessman serving a three-year sentence for bribery and corruption who was permitted to leave Jordan for medical treatment had disappeared. Khaled Shaheen had been incarcerated for his role in a bribery scandal over the upgrading of a state refinery.

- He had been permitted in February to leave for the United States for medical treatment but was then spotted in April 2011 at a London restaurant. He has subsequently disappeared and become a symbol of corruption in Jordan.

UNREST IN JORDAN

Dissent from within the King's Tribal Base

The deeply rooted political and economic frustration that has fueled revolution and widespread unrest across the Arab world since December 2010 has manifested itself in Jordan, shaking thelegitimacy of the Hashemite monarchy on a scale unseen in several decades. Though mass protests have yet to occur and there have been few instances of violent confrontation between protestors and the government, nevertheless public criticism of King Abdullah II, Queen Rania, and even the institution of monarchy has been unprecedented and has come from all sides, including from members of the kingdom's foundational support base—the tribal/military elite with roots around the East Bank of the Jordan River. Although some foreign observers watching unrest spread across the Arab world have been quick to argue that Arab kingdoms inherently are more stable than republics, it has been evident that no country in the Arab Middle East has been spared some form of domestic instability. Clearly, what are initially perceived as small incidentshave the potential to ignite public anger, and although this has yet to occ ur in Jordan, most experts would not discount the potential for more unrest there. In Jordan, like other countries in the Arab world, youth unemployment and underemployment are high, corruption is rampant, and socioeconomic mobility is limited.[6]

Protests emanating from the more rural, tribal areas of Jordan, traditionally considered government/military strongholds, have unnerved the monarchy. Even before the revolutions in Tunisia and Egypt, experts had warned that, particularly in 2010, tribal dissatisfaction was growing due to a lack of government investment in rural areas and anger against perceived corruption from within the inner circle of the royal family and its business allies.[7] In May 2010, a group reportedly representing thousands of East Bank retired soldiers known as the National Committee for Military Veterans (or National Committee of Military Retirees) issued a bold petition demanding that the king reverse liberal economic policies, curb corruption, and, most notably, disenfranchise Jordanian citizens who are of Palestinian origin.[8] In early January 2011, riots broke out in the southern town of Ma'an after an inter-tribal dispute over government employment became a larger protest against government neglect. In February 2011, tribal elites again criticized the monarchy when 36 prominent tribesmen issued a letter to the king, directly accusing Queen Rania of enriching her family and interfering in politics by promoting Palestinian allies. The letter demanded that farmlands rumored to have been sold to members of the queen's family be returned. It also criticized the queen for throwing herself a 40th birthday party in the famous desert preserve of Wadi Rum. The letter stated that "We reject outrageous birthdays that come at the expense of the poor and the treasury."[9] Also in February 2011, several tribes blocked a highway east of the capital, demanding the use of "tribal lands" which are government-owned but granted to the tribes for centuries. After receiving reassurances from the palace that their needs would be addressed, Faysal al Fayaz, head of the House of Representatives and a prominent member of the Bani Sakhar tribes, said, "We have never been forced to pledge allegiance or loyalty to the Hashemites because their actions have always been one step ahead of our aspirations."[10]

In Jordan, tribes of East Bank descent, the country's original inhabitants, make up the core of the military and the state bureaucracy. They are largely dependent on government patronage, which has been shrinking in recent years due to government efforts to rein in deficit spending. Tribesmen have vociferously protested against the privatization of state companies, accusing the royal family of not only selling off state lands but of undervaluing the sale of state potash and phosphate companies in deals with foreign corporations. According to one retired general who was a signatory to the 2010 petition from retired soldiers, "In one year, one [former state company] profited three times the sales price. This is not just corruption, it is audacious corruption."[11]

King Abdullah II has responded to tribal demands by increasing government patronage and spending and by appointing tribal loyalists to his administration. In a response to public anger, King Abdullah II directed his cabinet to cancel a sales tax imposed on fuel and reduced overall gas taxes. Subsidies for sugar and rice also were increased and public salaries have been raised. The full impact these measures will have on Jordan's public finances is uncertain. A draft 2011 budget had projected slowing public wage growth and still projected a deficit of over 5% of GDP.[12]

On February 1, 2011, King Abdullah II dismissed his government just several months after its formation, replacing Prime Minister Samir Rifai with Marouf al Bakhit, a former prime minister (2005 to 2007), general, and ambassador to Israel and Turkey.[13] Governments in Jordan typically last no more than 15 months (over the past 90 years, Amman has seen 72 different governments[14]), and the king may have acted to stem further criticism from his tribal base, as Bakhit is well regarded among various tribal leaders. In March 2011, the king also appointed as new chief to the royal court Khalid Karaki, a former royal court adviser and expert on tribal politics.

Youth-Driven Protests and Islamists

Criticism from the king's tribal base has quieted somewhat after youth protestors expanded their activism in March 2011. On Friday, March 24, several thousand Jordanian protestors (comprised of youth organizations, Islamists, leftists, and professional associations[15]) who were camped in central Amman clashed with government loyalists and police, leading to the death of 55-year-old Khairi Saad, who was killed after being beaten by security forces, though the government claims he died of a heart attack. In response to heightened protest, King Abdullah II has attempted to promote national unity and has engaged most but not all political forces in a national dialogue (the Jordanian Muslim Brotherhood has refused to participate).[16] He has also moved to amend the Public Gatherings Law[17] (requires preapproval for public demonstrations) and approved the formation of a Teachers Union.

Since March 24, an eponymous group calling itself the March 24 youth have held sit-ins and smaller protests outside state security, intelligence, and other government buildings. March 24 youth protestors have criticized the government's response to demonstrations, and one youth leader said that "We believe these changes are only cosmetic and don't address the core issues that need to be implemented right away — and that includes a Parliament and a government that represents the people.... We will continue our protests ... we will not be intimidated and we will continue to demand that reforms be implemented on the ground."[18] Young Jordanian protestors have been witnessed holding placards saying that "I am no longer a sheep," but no other largescale, violent incidents have been reported. In order to prevent violence, the government has designated specific areas for protest. On April 6, 2011, 200 public figures signed a statement condemning the violence used against protestors on March 24. The document was signed by a former prime minister as well as many other former ministers, union members, and tribal leaders. In mid-April 2011, 77 members of the "Youth of March 24" were tried before a military court for "public order offences" resulting from the violence of March 24, 2011.

In Amman, the Jordanian Muslim Brotherhood and its political action wing, the Islamic Action Front (IAF), have been part of these protests and have demanded the dissolution of the government, the dissolution of parliament, the holding of new elections under a revised electoral law, and the amending of the constitution to allow for the direct election of the prime minister. However, Islamists are not calling for the overthrow of the monarchy. According to IAF Secretary-General Hamzah Mansur, "There is no comparison between Egypt and Jordan. The people there demand a regime change, but here we ask for political reforms and an elected government."

On Friday, April 15, ultra-conservative Islamists in the city of Zarqa carried out a demonstration calling for the release of other Islamist prisoners. The government claims that the demonstrators then attacked police with swords, daggers, and clubs, resulting in several injuries and the detainment of 70 Islamists. Among the detained was Ayman al Balawi, the brother of Humam Khalil Abu Mulal al Balawi, who killed eight CIA employees in Afghanistan in December 2009 (see footnote 66).

The King's Dilemma

Since the founding of the kingdom in 1946, successive Jordanian monarchs have had to balance the competing needs of their domestic constituents and foreign alliances, and the broad political change sweeping across the Arab world has strained this delicate process. King Abdullah II needs to satisfy his tribal East Bank base, which seeks state patronage and fears that a democratic Jordan would become a state dominated by Arabs of Palestinian origin. At the same time, the king must promote national unity, champion Jordan's "progressive" image abroad, and manage an economy that currently is unable to generate enough private sector jobs, thereby leading to unsustainable budget deficits as the state attempts to fill the void.[19] In the past, King Abdullah II tried to remain above the fray and place blame on his cabinet subordinates or Jordan's weak parliament for the lack of reform and economic development. However, regional developments have negated this strategy, and the king may be forced to implement real reforms in order to stave off greater unrest. To date, this has not happened in any meaningful way.

On the other hand, many experts believe that Jordanians themselves, while unhappy with the status quo, are unwilling to completely change the political system due to fear of unleashing societal tensions that are kept at bay by the very monarchy many protestors have decried. According to Nathan J. Brown, a Middle East expert at the Carnegie Endowment for International Peace,

In a society in which citizens cannot choose a soccer team to support without betraying their origin (East Bank Jordanians versus Palestinians) and all too often coming to blows, any political change is evaluated on Jordanian-Palestinian lines. A common platform of political reform is difficult to develop in such a context. While Egyptians shouted "Leave!" and "Get out!" to their president, Jordanians are far more likely to fear what would come next if their king abdicated. An Islamist firebrand told me directly that he is now pulling his rhetorical punches because he does not want to create another Lebanon.[20]

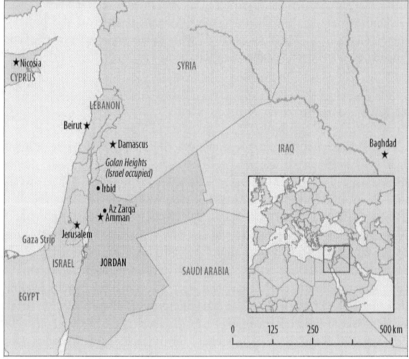

Source: CRS Graphics.

Figure 1. Jordan and Its Neighbors.

COUNTRY OVERVIEW

Although the United States and Jordan have never been linked by a formal treaty, they have cooperated on a number of regional and international issues for decades. The country's small size and lack of major economic resources have made it dependent on aid from Western and friendly Arab sources. U.S. support, in particular, has helped Jordan deal with serious vulnerabilities, both internal and external. Jordan's geographic position, wedged between Israel, Syria, Iraq, and Saudi Arabia, has made it vulnerable to the strategic designs of its more powerful neighbors, but has also given Jordan an important role as a buffer between these potential adversaries. In 1990, Jordan's unwillingness to join the allied coalition against Iraq disrupted its relations with the United States and the Persian Gulf states; however, relations improved throughout the 1990s as Jordan played an increasing role in the Arab-Israeli peace process and distanced itself from the Iraqi regime of Saddam Hussein.

DOMESTIC POLITICS AND THE ECONOMY

Jordan, created by colonial powers after World War I, initially consisted of desert or semi-desert territory east of the Jordan River, inhabited largely by people of Bedouin tribal background. The establishment of the state of Israel brought large numbers of Palestinian refugees to Jordan, which subsequently annexed a small Palestinian enclave west of the Jordan River. The original "East Bank" Jordanians, though probably no longer a majority in Jordan, remain predominant in the country's political and military establishments and form the bedrock of support for the Jordanian monarchy. Jordanians of Palestinian origin comprise an estimated 55% to 70% of the population and generally tend to gravitate toward the private sector due to their exclusion from certain public sector and military positions.[21]

The Hashemite Royal Family

Jordan is a hereditary constitutional monarchy under the prestigious Hashemite family, which claims descent from the Prophet Muhammad. King Abdullah II has ruled the country since 1999, when he succeeded to the throne upon the death of his father, the late King Hussein, after a 47-year reign. Educated largely in Britain and the United States, King Abdullah II had earlier pursued a military career, ultimately serving as commander of Jordan's Special Operations Forces with the rank of Major General. The king's 15-year-old son Prince Hussein is the designated crown prince.[22]

JORDAN IN BRIEF

Population: 6,407,085 (July 2010 est.)
Area: 89,213 sq. km. (34,445 sq. mi., slightly smaller than Indiana)
Ethnic Groups: Arabs 98%; Circassians 1%; Armenians 1%
Religion: Sunni Muslim 92%; Christian 6%; small Muslim sects 2%
(2001 est.)
Literacy: 89% (male 95%, female 84%) (2003 est.)
GDP: Per Capita $5,300 (2010 est.)
Inflation: 4.4% (2010 CIA est.) 5.5%
(December 2010 IMF est.)
Unemployment: 13.5% (official estimate); ca. 30% according to some
unofficial estimates (2009 est.)
External Debt: $5.52 billion (December 2010 est.)
Sources: U.S. Dept. of State; CIA World Factbook; Central Bank of
Jordan; International Monetary Fund, other U.S. and Jordanian government
departments; The Economist Intelligence Unit (London)

King Abdullah II (age 49) has won approval for his energetic and hands-on style of governing; however, some Jordanians, notably Palestinians and Islamic fundamentalists, are opposed to his policies of cooperating with the United States on issues such as Iraq and the Arab-Israeli peace process.

The king appoints a prime minister to head the government and the Council of Ministers (cabinet). Typically, Jordanian governments last no more than 15 months before they are dissolved by royal decree. This is done in order to bolster the king's reform credentials and to dispense patronage to various elites. The king also appoints all judges and is commander of the armed forces.

Parliament, Constitution, and Elections

Jordan's bicameral legislature is composed of a mostly elected 120-member lower house and an appointed 55-member upper house.[23] Building on his father's legacy, King Abdullah II has supported a limited parliamentary democracy, while periodically curtailing dissent when it threatened economic reforms or normalization of relations with Israel. Overall, parliament has limited power. In theory, it can override the veto authority of the king with a two-thirds majority in both the upper and lower houses. A two-thirds majority of the lower house can also dissolve the cabinet with a "no confidence" vote. However, since both houses almost always have solid progovernment majorities, such actions are rarely attempted (once in April 1963). The constitution enables the king to dissolve parliament and postpone lower house elections for two years.[24] The king also can circumvent parliament through a constitutional mechanism that allows provisional legislation to be issued by the cabinet when parliament is not sitting or has been dissolved.[25] The king also can issue royal decrees, which are not subject to parliamentary scrutiny.

Overall, political parties in Jordan are extremely weak, as the moderately fundamentalist Islamic Action Front (IAF) is the only well-organized movement. Most parties represent narrow parochial interests and are composed of prominent individuals representing a particular family or tribe. There are approximately 36 small parties in Jordan, consisting of an estimated 4,100 total members.[26]

The 1993 Election Law

The opposition in Jordan routinely criticizes the law governing national elections. After Islamists made gains in the 1989 parliamentary elections, the government changed[27] the rules to a "one man, one vote" system that gives citizens one vote regardless of how many parliamentary seats represent their district.[28] When forced to choose just one representative, voters have typically chosen candidates based on familial or tribal ties—not on ideology. Reformers would like to see a mixed election system that provides for some proportional representation and allows parties to field lists of candidates. In addition, many reformers have called for changes to Jordan's electoral map, asserting that the government gerrymandered voting districts to favor candidates from rural tribal strongholds over urban areas where Islamists typically have more support.[29]

2010 Parliamentary Elections

In late 2009, King Abdullah II dissolved parliament two years before scheduled parliamentary elections. A month later, he appointed 43-year-old Samir al Rifai as prime minister. Shortly thereafter, Al Rifai formed a new cabinet, and the king instructed Rifai to implement economic reforms, hold new parliamentary elections in 2010 under a new election law, and clamp down on corruption.

In May 2010, the king passed by royal decree (with cabinet approval) a new temporary electoral law to govern parliamentary elections set for November 9, 2010. The law makes minor modifications to the 1993 electoral law without addressing the fundamental grievances of opposition critics, who charge that the old and new laws both favor rural, pro-royal constituencies over urban, Islamist-leaning areas. The Jordanian Muslim Brotherhood's political party, the Islamic Action Front (IAF), threatened to boycott the elections.

The new law raises the number of lower house seats from 110 to 120. Of the 10 new seats, 6 are allocated for women under the existing quota system (raising the number of quota seats from 6 to 12), and the remaining 4 are distributed to districts representing the cities of Amman, Zarqa, and Irbid. The government claims that by adding seats to underrepresented urban areas, it is responding to calls for reform. The government also claims that the new law stiffens penalties for election-related violations, such as using money to influence voting.

The new electoral law preserves the "one-man, one-vote system." It also creates 45 electoral zones, which in turn contain a total of 108 sub-districts, with each sub-district sitting one member of parliament. The remaining 12 seats are set aside for the women's quota. Voters are registered in the larger electoral zone and may vote for only one candidate in the given sub-district of their choice. Candidates must choose to run in one sub-district.

According to one analysis of the new law, "with smaller sub-districts, candidates will now rely more on their tribal affiliations and campaign among a smaller pool of core familial voters than before."[30] Another expert asserts that "The new system also opens the possibility that a loser in one sub-district may have won more votes than the winner in another sub-district. This oddity of Jordan's new system means that a given electoral district might be represented in Parliament by one or more politicians who were not among the top vote-getters in the district."[31]

Most foreign observers of Jordanian domestic politics believe that internal fissures over what constitutes Jordan's national identity are the main factor inhibiting democracy there. In this context, the ruling Hashemite family and its allies of East Bank tribal elites are unwilling to cede power to Jordanians of Palestinian origin, some of whom fill the ranks of the Muslim Brotherhood. At the same time, fears of Palestinians in the West Bank being pushed into Jordan as the result of a failed peace process drive the government's inability to open up the political system. According to Jordan expert Professor Curtis Ryan:

The 2010 elections will be contested in a way that, despite the minor reforms, should minimize the development of political parties and encourage localized rather than national voting. It should also ensure a parliament that is once again largely elected based on tribal linkages, far outweighing whatever strength the democratic opposition is able to muster.... The battle over the new election law, like so much in Jordanian politics, is permeated by the demographic and political battles over the role of its citizens of Palestinian origin and the prospects of an eventual Palestinian state.[32]

The November 2010 election transpired as expected. The IAF boycotted the election and only 17 opposition members were elected, leaving the government with an overwhelming majority in parliament. Some violent incidents occurred, though foreign observers praised the conduct of authorities. According to the U.S. State Department,

> We were pleased to review the preliminary reports released on November 10 by the International Republican Institute (IRI) and the National Democratic Institute (NDI) in which IRI deemed the Jordanian elections as "credible" and "a significant improvement for the Middle East" and NDI found that "the conduct of voting on election day compared favorably to accepted international practices" and the process showed a "clear improvement over the election process in 2007."....In line with the full scope of their missions, both NDI and IRI identified a number of areas for improvement that, if addressed, would further increase citizen confidence in the electoral process. While there were sporadic incidents of violence on election day, as well as reports of a number of irregularities in the administration of the election, IRI noted that the balloting process was generally calm and orderly.[33]

The Jordanian Muslim Brotherhood

The Jordanian Muslim Brotherhood has long been integrated into the political mainstream due to its acceptance of the legitimacy of the Hashemite monarchy, although relations between the Brotherhood and the palace have fluctuated over the years. The Brotherhood presence in Jordan dates back to the 1930s, as it has been tacitly recognized first as a charitable organization and later as a quasi-political organization, which has openly fielded candidates in parliamentary elections albeit under a different name (Islamic Action Front, IAF). The relationship between the Brotherhood and the palace has been mutually beneficial over the years. Successive Jordanian monarchs have found that the Brotherhood has been more useful politically as an ally than as an opponent (as opposed to the Brotherhood in Egypt), as it secured Islamist support in countering Arab nationalist interference during the 1950s and 1960s and secular Palestinian nationalism in the 1970s. The Brotherhood's educational, social, and health services have grown so extensive over the years that some experts believe that the Brotherhood's budget for services rivals that of the Jordanian government.

Like other Islamist parties in the region, the Islamic Action Front, the Muslim Brotherhood's political wing, operates in a tight political space, wedged between a government which seeks to limit its influence and a disillusioned constituency impatient for reform. In Jordan's poorer neighborhoods, the Brotherhood uses its social services to attract support, though it must compete with the growing allure of militant Islam, emanating both from within Jordan and from neighboring Iraq. The IAF markets itself as beyond the culture of corruption found in Jordanian politics, and while this message may resonate with the average supporter, it is unclear what the party's platform is aside from its slogan of "Islam is the solution."

With the government seeking to limit its activities and having performed poorly in the 2007 parliamentary elections, the Brotherhood reorganized in 2008 and internally elected Dr. Hamam Said (alternate spellings: Himman Said/Hammam Sa'id /Hamam Sa'id/Hammam Saaed) as the movement's new general guide. Press reports have described the leader as a "hawk," stressing his Palestinian origins and possible ties to Hamas.

The Military and Security Establishment

Many tribal East Bank Jordanians or their descendants form the backbone of Jordan's armed forces and internal security establishment. Most observers agree that with the possible exception of Syria, Jordan faces few conventional threats from its neighbors and that the greatest threats to its security are internal and asymmetrical. In general, counter-terrorism and homeland security policies are carried out by a number of institutions, most notably the security services under direct palace control, the military, and the Interior Ministry. The General Intelligence Directorate (GID) reports directly to King Abdullah II and is responsible for both covert operations abroad and internal security. The military's elite special forces units also are directly involved in countering threats to internal security and were reportedly used to thwart a chemical weapons plot in April 2004. The Interior Ministry controls all civilian police forces and civil defense units through a branch agency known as the Public Security Directorate (PSD).

The Economy

With few natural resources[34] and a small industrial base, Jordan has an economy which is heavily dependent on external aid from abroad, tourism, expatriate worker remittances,[35] and the service sector. Among the long-standing problems Jordan faces are poverty (15%-30%), corruption, slow economic growth, and high levels of unemployment, nominally around 13% but thought by many analysts to be in the 25%-30% range.[36] Corruption[37] is particularly pronounced in Jordan. Use of intermediaries, referred to in Arabic as *"Wasta"* (connections), is widespread, and many young Jordanians have grown frustrated by the lack of social and economic mobility that corruption engenders. Each year, thousands of Jordanians go abroad in search of better jobs and opportunities. Like many poor countries, Jordan suffers from a "brain drain" of its most talented workers, and the government has struggled to develop incentives to keep its well-educated, highly skilled workers close to home. The government is by far the largest employer with between onethird and two-thirds of all workers on the state's payroll.

Water Shortages

Jordan is one of the 10 most water-deprived countries in the world and is in constant search of new water resources. Most of the country's drinking water is secured from underground wells, and excessive pumping over decades has led water levels to drop precipitously. The agricultural sector uses an estimated 60% to 70% of all water resources, but only accounts for about 3% of GDP. A series of recent droughts has exacerbated existing shortages, and experts have warned that the kingdom's overall water situation is deteriorating.

In addition, the Dead Sea, which abuts both Jordan and Israel, is losing water at an estimated 3 feet per year, and some scientists suggest that without significant action it will be gone by 2050. Jordan has been exploring new water development projects, including the feasibility of pumping water from the Red Sea, desalinating it, and then transferring it north and down below sea level tothe Dead Sea. This project, referred to as the Red-Dead Canal, is being studied by the government and international lenders.

Civilian Nuclear Energy Program

In order to address chronic water and energy shortages, Jordan would need energy-intensive desalination plants and the electric power to fuel them. For the past three years, the kingdom has moved ahead with plans to develop a domestic civilian nuclear energy program. In a January 2007 interview with an Israeli newspaper, King Abdullah II announced his country's plans to construct a nuclear-powered reactor for peaceful purposes. Most analysts believe that Jordan, like other Arab countries, is using the specter of a looming Iranian nuclear threat to generate international support for a nuclear program which, in Jordan's case, would mainly alleviate electricity and fuel shortages needed to power new desalination plants. Between 2017 and 2030, the government aims to have between 20% and 30% of its annual electricity generated by nuclear power. Nonetheless, financing a nuclear program may be cost prohibitive without significant international support. In September 2007 at a nuclear energy summit in Vienna, Austria, the United States and Jordan signed a memorandum of understanding outlining potential U.S.-Jordanian co-operation on developing requirements for appropriate power reactors, fuel service arrangements, civilian training, nuclear safety, and energy technology. In 2008, the United States agreed to supply Jordan with radiation monitors at the kingdom's border crossings to foil any illegal trafficking of nuclear materials.

To date, Jordan has made substantial progress in securing international private sector and governmental support for its nuclear plans. In 2008, the Jordan Atomic Energy Commission (JAEC) signed a uranium[38] exploration agreement with the French company Areva for joint exploration of uranium in central Jordan. Several months later, JAEC signed a memorandum of understanding (MoU) covering exploration and mining of uranium and other ores with British- Australian mining company Rio Tinto. In 2009, Jordan signed a $173 million deal[39] with the state-run South Korean Atomic Energy Research Institute and Daewoo Engineering and Construction Co. to construct a 5-megawatt nuclear reactor at the Jordan University for Sciencesand Technology near the northern city of Irbid. The reactor facility is to be used to train Jordanianstaff. Also in 2009, Jordan signed another agreement with Areva granting the French company the exclusive right to extract and mine uranium in central Jordan.

There are still a number of obstacles to clear before Jordan can begin construction on any largescale reactor, including determining its location, its cost, and what role, if any, the United States may play in providing technical assistance. Jordan's coastline may be too small for a reactor facility and any attempt to place it further inland may have to contend with the challenge of piping and pumping water uphill to a power plant. Some Israeli officials are concerned that a potential Jordanian nuclear power plant could be built too close to the Dead Sea Rift, an area prone to earthquakes. Israeli officials assert that an earthquake could cause radioactive leaks that could then damage the nearby Israeli city Eilat. They have asked the Jordanian government to locate any reactor in a more geologically stable location, such as the cliffs above the coastal southern city of Aqaba.[40] Financing Jordan's ambitious program also is a major obstacle, as estimates run into the billions of dollars. To date, four companies are in competition to build the main reactor. They include Korea Electric Power Corporation (KEPCO), the prime contractor for the United Arab Emirates; Areva, the French company; Atomic Energy of Canada; and AtomStroyExport of Russia.

Jordanian public opinion, like in many countries, has somewhat turned against the pursuit of nuclear energy since the crisis unfolded at the Fukushima Daiichi nuclear power plant in Japan beginning in March 2011. Small groups of protestors have rallied outside government buildings, chanting "no to nuclear power" and Jordanian media reports indicate that activists are attempting to obtain 100,000 signatures on a petition calling for the end of Jordan's pursuit of nuclear power.

U.S.-Jordanian Nuclear Cooperation: Negotiations over a 123 Agreement

The United States is a major political and financial supporter of the Jordanian government, and Jordan is intent on securing U.S. technical and financial backing of its nascent nuclear project. However, both sides are currently at odds over Jordan's desire to maintain its right to enrich its own domestically mined uranium, one of the rare natural resources found in the kingdom. The process of uranium ore enrichment for fuel also can be used to produce weapons-grade materials. As such, the Obama Administration has continued the Bush Administration approach of seeking to limit the adoption of uranium enrichment technology among other countries in order to limit the potential spread of expertise or materials that could be used to build nuclear weapons. On the other hand, the Jordanian government insists it has a right to enrich its own domestic uranium resources and officials have pledged to send uranium-ore deposits abroad for processing into nuclear fuels.

By law, all U.S. nuclear cooperation with foreign countries requires, under Section 123 of the Atomic Energy Act of 1954, a peaceful nuclear cooperation agreement. Once an agreement is signed, Jordan would be eligible to receive U.S. nuclear equipment, fuel, and expertise. However, the U.S. government would like Jordan to sign a 123 agreement that closely resembles its 2009 agreement with the United Arab Emirates (UAE) that, among many other provisions, stated:

The UAE "shall not possess sensitive nuclear facilities within its territory or otherwise engage in activities within its territory for, or relating to, the enrichment or reprocessing of material, or for the alternation in form or content (except by irradiation or further irradiation or, if agreed by the Parties, post-irradiation examination) of plutonium, uranium 233, high enriched uranium, or irradiated source or special fissionable material."[41]

In April 2010, Chairman of the Jordanian Atomic Energy Commission Khalid Touqan said that "Jordan upholds its right to enrich uranium under the accords of the Nuclear Non-Proliferation Treaty and the supervision of the International Atomic Energy Agency."[42] Jordan signed the Non- Proliferation Treaty in 1968 and ratified an Additional Protocol with the International Atomic Energy Agency (IAEA) in 1998. According to one report, the Obama Administration is seeking guarantees that Jordan won't enrich uranium domestically, fearing that the UAE, under the terms of its deal, could demand a renegotiation if another Middle Eastern country secures an agreement with the United States under more favorable terms.[43]

For months, U.S.-Jordanian negotiations have remained at an impasse. In an interview with the *Wall Street Journal*, King Abdullah II blamed Israel for lobbying against any U.S.-Jordanian nuclear deal, saying that "there are countries, Israel in particular, that are more worried about us being economically independent than the issue of nuclear energy, and have been voicing their concerns.... There are many such reactors in the world and a lot more coming, so [the Israelis must] go mind their own business."[44]

However, in late 2010 Jordanian officials appeared more optimistic about a possible compromise solution. During a one-day visit to Jordan in September 2010, Secretary of State Hillary Rodham Clinton held a press conference with Foreign Minister Nasser Judeh. During the proceedings, the foreign minister hinted at a possible U.S.-Jordanian compromise when he remarked:

On bilateral relations, I would like to say that this strategic relationship between us gets stronger by the day. We thank the United States for its support for Jordan on all levels. In my most recent meeting with the Secretary in Washington a couple of weeks ago, or just under a couple of weeks ago, we made serious headway on a range of issues. Particularly, I mentioned the nuclear cooperation agreement which is under discussion and hopefully nearing the end of that discussion, and we thank the United States for its strong and firm support for Jordan on that front.[45]

In late September 2010, Jordanian officials publicly indicated that a possible compromise U.S.- Jordanian nuclear deal was on the horizon. Reportedly, Jordan has agreed to mine uranium but not enrich it. According to one Jordanian official, "We received a positive gesture from the U.S. administration, and we are hoping to reach a compromise and sign the agreement by the end of this year.... Our official strategic plan is not to enrich uranium now, but in the future this may change, so we will not give up our right to do so."[46]

CURRENT ISSUES IN U.S.-JORDANIAN RELATIONS

Promoting Peace in the Middle East

Finding a peaceful solution to the Israeli-Palestinian conflict is the utmost priority of the Jordanian government. Although Jordan joined other neighboring Arab states in a series of military conflicts against Israel between 1948 and 1973, the late King Hussein (ruled 1952-1999) ultimately concluded that peace with Israel was in Jordan's strategic interests due to Israel's conventional military superiority, the development of an independent Palestinian national movement that threatened both Jordanian and Israeli security, and Jordan's support for Saddam Hussein in the first Gulf War, which isolated it from the West.[47] Consequently, in 1994 Jordan and Israel signed a peace treaty,[48] and King Abdullah II has used his country's semi-cordial official relationship with Israel to improve Jordan's standing with Western governments and international financial institutions, on which it relies heavily for external support and aid.

Nevertheless, the continuation of conflict continues to be a major obstacle to Jordan's development. The issue of Palestinian rights resonates with much of the population, as more than half of all Jordanian citizens originate from either the West Bank or the pre-1967 borders of Israel. There are an estimated 1.9 million United Nations-registered Palestinian refugees in Jordan, and, while many no longer regard their stay in Jordan as temporary, they have retained their refugee status both as a symbolic sign of support for Palestinians living under Israeli occupation and in hope of being included in any future settlement.[49] Furthermore, for King Abdullah II and the royal Hashemite family, who are of Arab Bedouin descent and rely politically on the support of East Bank tribal families, finding a solution to the conflict is considered a matter of political survival since the government cannot afford to ignore an issue of critical importance to a majority of its citizens. The royal family and their tribal constituents vehemently reject periodic Israeli calls for the reunification of the West Bank with Jordan proper (dubbed the "Jordanian Option"), a maneuver that could inevitably alter the political status quo in Jordan. Like his father before him, King Abdullah II has

Opposition to Normalization

King Abdullah's efforts to normalize relations with Israel have faced significant resistance within Jordan, particularly among Islamic fundamentalist groups, parts of the Palestinian community, and influential trade and professional organizations. Among many mainstream Jordanians, there is some disappointment that peace with Israel has not brought more tangible economic benefits to them so far. Opponents of normalization have repeatedly called on Jordanians to boycott contacts with Israel, and activists among them have compiled "black lists" of Jordanian individuals and companies that deal with Israel. The Jordanian government has arrested organizers of these lists, but courts have upheld their right to publish them. In addition, IAF parliamentarians periodically propose legislation to prohibit cooperation with Israel in various sectors. The IAF also has proposed legislation to abrogate Jordan's 1994 peace treaty with Israel.

Reviving the Arab-Israeli Peace Process

For nearly a decade, King Abdullah II has attempted to convince U.S. policy makers and Congress to become more actively involved in mediating between Israelis and Palestinians. King Abdullah II is a strong supporter of a Saudi initiative, dubbed the "Arab Peace Initiative," which calls for Israel's full withdrawal from all occupied territories and the establishment of a Palestinian state in the West Bank and Gaza Strip in exchange for full normalization of relations with all Arab states in the region. In a March 2007 address to a joint session of Congress, King Abdullah II pleaded for U.S. leadership in the peace process, which he called the "core issue in the Middle East." He suggested that the Arab Peace Initiative is a path to achieve a collective peace treaty. Jordanian officials also have repeatedly condemned Israeli settlement activities in the West Bank, especially in Jerusalem, claiming that they violate international law and heightentensions in the region.

In July 2010, Israeli Prime Minister Benjamin Netanyahu made a surprise visit to Jordan for meetings with King Abdullah II. Reportedly, Netanyahu sought Jordanian support for direct Israeli-Palestinian talks, and both sides may have sought to improve relations in what has been a notably tense period.

Several months earlier, King Abdullah II had stated in a *Wall Street Journal* article that "for the first time since my father made peace with Israel, our relationship with Israel is at an all bottom low. It hasn't been as bad as it is today and as tense as it is today."

In September 2010, King Abdullah II traveled to Washington, DC, for the launch of U.S.- brokered peace negotiations between the Palestinians and Israel. A month later, the king told Israeli Prime Minister Benjamin Netanyahu that "all unilateral actions that threaten peace, in particular the construction of settlements, must cease."

Jordan-Hamas Relations

For two decades, Jordan has had an on-again, off-again relationship with Hamas, the Palestinian militant group and U.S. State Department-designated Foreign Terrorist Organization (FTO). Throughout the 1990s, the late King Hussein tolerated a Hamas presence in his kingdom.[50] Upon his accession to the throne in 1999, King Abdullah II, perhaps realizing that Jordan's relationship with Hamas was a political liability, reversed his late father's long -standing policy of tolerating Hamas and closed its Jordan offices permanently.

Since then, Jordan has been a strong backer of Palestinian moderates (such as the Fatah party) loyal to President Mahmoud Abbas and has been determined to bolster the capacity of the Palestinian Authority (PA) in the West Bank in order to prevent Hamas from gaining strength there. Jordan has provided training for several battalions of U.S.-screened Palestinian recruits to serve in an overhauled Palestinian Authority National Security Force.[51] The training is conducted by Jordanian police at the Jordanian International Police Training Center near Amman.

Toward the end of 2008, perhaps in order to hedge against the prospect of yet another round of failed Israeli-Palestinian peace negotiations, Jordan opened a dialogue with Hamas officials. Led by General Muhammad Dahabi, Jordan reportedly discussed "political and security issues" with their Hamas counterparts (Muhammad Nazzal). Most analysts interpreted this limited engagement as a pragmatic Jordanian maneuver designed to open channels of communication with an emboldened Hamas now in firm control of the Gaza Strip. Jordan may have sought a pledge from Hamas not to interfere in Jordanian domestic politics. According to one observer, "Hamas wants to talk with Jordan and Jordan wants to listen to what Hamas has to say. And it is in Jordan's interest today to communicate with all and sundry—north, south, east, and west, without changing the underlying fundamentals of its policies, instead of concentrating on an alliance with only two states, the United States and Israel."[52]

Since the 2006 Hamas victory in Palestinian Authority legislative elections, the Jordanian government has been placed in a difficult position. Much of its citizenry sympathizes with Hamas, and Jordan's own Islamist party, the Islamic Action Front (IAF), reportedly maintains close ties to Hamas. The IAF has been careful to downplay these ties and, in August 2009, three high-ranking moderate Brotherhood figures resigned from the group's leadership bureau in protest over Hamas-Jordanian Brotherhood ties. According to one IAF statement, "Abbas is the legitimate Palestinian president and Hamas's battle should be with the Zionist enemy, not other Palestinians, so we ask them to return to a policy of dialogue and to restore the institutions in Gaza."[53] Some critics of King Abdullah II assert that the Hamas threat to Jordan is a specter used by the royal family to consolidate its rule and repress potential opposition.

Terrorism

Jordan is a key partner in fighting international Islamic terrorist groups, as its main intelligence organization, the General Intelligence Directorate (GID), is considered one of the most effective organizations in the region at infiltrating Jihadist networks.[54] Jordanian intelligence reportedly played a role in assisting U.S. forces in killing Abu Musab al Zarqawi, the fugitive Jordanian terrorist mastermind who headed the Al Qaeda in Iraq organization until his death in June 2006. Zarqawi hailed from the industrial town of Zarqa, several miles northeast of Amman, which is known as a source of Sunni militancy, as dozens of its young men have traveled to Iraq to die as suicide bombers. According to one Islamist community leader in Zarqa, "Most of the young people here in Zarqa are very religious.... And when they see the news and what is going on in the Islamic countries, they themselves feel that they have to go to fight jihad. Today, you don't need anyone to tell the young men that they should go to jihad. They themselves want to be martyrs."

Jordan's cooperative relationship with the United States has made it vulnerable to terrorist attacks, particularly from organizations operating from Iraq. On November 9, 2005, near simultaneous explosions at three Western-owned hotels in Amman (the Radisson, Grand Hyatt, and Days Inn) killed 58 persons and seriously wounded approximately 100 others. The terrorist organization Al Qaeda in Iraq, formerly headed by Zarqawi, claimed responsibility for the act. Many Jordanians, even some who disagree with their government's support for U.S. Middle East policies, have condemned the hotel bombings, which killed many Jordanians, and denounced Zarqawi's actions. King Abdullah II has said the attacks were aimed at ordinary Jordanians, not foreigners, noting that the hotels, though Western owned, were frequented by local citizens. On November 15, 2005, Jordan's minister of the interior announced new security regulations designed to keep foreign militants from operating covertly in Jordan, including a requirement for Jordanians to notify authorities within 48 hours of renting an apartment or a house to foreigners.

Other terrorist activity in Jordan includes the following:

- On October 28, 2002, Lawrence Foley, a U.S. diplomat assigned to the U.S. Agency for International Development (USAID) program in Jordan, was shot and killed by an unknown assailant as Foley was leaving for work from his residence. A Jordanian military court convicted and sentenced to death eight Islamic militants linked to Al Qaeda and presumably involved in the Foley murder; the court sentenced two others to jail terms and acquitted one defendant. Six of the eight sentenced to death were tried *in absentia*, including Zarqawi, and two more were executed on March 11, 2006.
- In April 2004, Jordanian authorities reportedly uncovered a plot by a terrorist cell linked to Zarqawi which planned to launch a chemical attack in the Jordanian capital of Amman. According to press reports, in January 2004, one of the would be perpetrators visited Iraq, where he obtained $170,000, which Zarqawi had collected from Syrian donors to pay for the attack. The plot was reportedly foiled by Jordanian police and elite special forces units in a series of operations in Amman.
- On August 19, 2005, rockets apparently aimed at two U.S. amphibious warfare ships visiting the Jordanian port of Aqaba narrowly missed their targets, one hitting a nearby warehouse and another landing near a hospital; a third rocket struck near the airport at the neighboring Israeli port of Eilat. A Jordanian soldier was killed and another injured in the attack. There were two claims of responsibility, both from groups believed to be affiliated with Zarqawi.
- On September 4, 2006, a lone gunman opened fire on a group of Western tourists visiting the historic Roman amphitheater in downtown Amman, killing a British man and wounding six others,

including a Jordanian policeman. The assailant was a 38-year-old Jordanian named Nabeel Jaoura, who claimed his attack was in retaliation for the murder of his two brothers in 1982 at the hands of Israeli soldiers during the war in southern Lebanon. According to the *New York Times*, Jaoura had worked in Israel, where he was arrested two years ago for overstaying his visa. Jordanian security officials believe his incarceration may have further radicalized him.[55]

- In late 2006, Jordanian intelligence authorities thwarted a potential bomb attack against foreign tourists traveling through Queen Alia Airport in Amman. Several of the convicted conspirators were Iraqis, and one of the ringleaders of the plot reportedly had sought to place a bomb in a sports bag using the explosive PE-4A, which is used by insurgents in Iraq.

- In September 2009, a Jordanian citizen who was living in the United States illegally was arrested and charged with attempting to blow up a skyscraper in Dallas, TX. Hosam Maher Husein Smadi, age 19, was arrested after planting an inert bomb at Fountain Place, a 60-story glass tower in downtown Dallas following an undercover FBI operation. Smadi was sentenced to 24 years in prison.

- In January 2010, a roadside bomb exploded near an Israeli Embassy vehicle travelling from Amman toward the border with Israel. There were no reports of injuries.

- In August 2010, several Chinese-made Grad-type rockets fired from Egypt's Sinai desert struck the Jordanian town of Aqaba, killing a taxi driver and wounding four others. Israel, Egypt, and Jordan all have disagreed over the attack's perpetrators. Israel and Egypt claim that Hamas may have fired the rocket intending to hit Israel, while Jordan claims that the attackers may have been from a branch of Al Qaeda based in the Gaza Strip.

Allegations of Torture

As media scrutiny over the CIA's alleged practice of transporting terrorism suspects to detention facilities abroad has grown in recent years, Jordan's General Intelligence Department (GID) has been accused of detaining and torturing CIA prisoners captured in other countries. According to a *Washington Post* article on the GID, "its [GID's] interrogators had a reputation for persuading tight-lipped suspects to talk, even if that meant using abusive tactics that could violate U.S. or international law."[56] In July 2006, the human rights group Amnesty International accused the Jordanian security establishment of torturing terrorist suspects on behalf of the United States government. Amnesty International identified 10 suspected cases of men subjected to rendition from U.S. custody to interrogation centers in Jordan.[57] A second report, released by Human Rights Watch in September 2006, claimed that the GID carries out arbitrary arrests and abuses suspects in its own detention facility. The report studied the cases of 16 men whom the GID had arrested and found that in 14 of the 16 cases, detainees were tortured or ill-treated. In response, the GID denied any wrongdoing. Finally, in a January 2007 report, Manfred Nowak, the United Nations Special Rapporteur on Torture and Other Cruel, Inhuman or Degrading Treatment or Punishment, concluded that "the practice of torture persists in Jordan because of a lack of awareness of the problem, and because of institutionalized impunity." In April 2008, three prisoners were killed and dozens of others injured during a riot at Muwaqqar prison. According to the Jordanian National Centre for Human Rights (NCHR), "mistreatment and beatings of inmates by some policemen at the Muaqqar prison led to the rioting."

Despite government denials or statements suggesting that reforms are underway, international monitoring groups continue to charge that torture in the Jordanian prison system is widespread. An October 2008 Human Rights Watch report alleged that despite an amendment to the penalcode to make torture a crime, Jordan's measures have been insufficient and the practice continues. According to Sarah Leah Whitson, Middle East director at Human Rights Watch, "Torture in Jordan's prison system is widespread even two years after King Abdullah II called for reforms to stop it once and for all.... The mechanisms for preventing torture by holding torturers accountable are simply not working."[58]

U.S. Aid, Trade, and Military Cooperation

U.S. Foreign Assistance to Jordan

The United States has provided economic and military aid, respectively, to Jordan since 1951 and 1957. Total U.S. aid to Jordan through FY2011 amounted to approximately $12.47 billion. Jordan has received large allocations in subsequent supplemental appropriations acts (a total of $2.186 billion since FY2002). In addition to funds specifically earmarked for Jordan, emergency supplemental bills also have contained funds to reimburse

Pakistan, Jordan, and other key cooperation states for logistical expenses in support of U.S. military operations.

The Five-Year Aid Deal

On September 22, 2008, the U.S. and Jordanian governments reached an agreement whereby the United States will provide a total of $660 million in annual foreign assistance to Jordan over a five-year period (FY2010-FY2014). Under the terms of their non-binding Memorandum of Understanding (MOU), this first-of-its-kind deal commits the United States, subject to future congressional appropriation and availability of funds, to providing $360 million per year in Economic Support Funds (ESF) and $300 million per year in Foreign Military Financing (FMF).[59] According to the Jordanian government, the agreement "reaffirms the strategic partnership and cooperation between the two countries." At a time when the overall budget for foreign aid has been constrained by U.S. operations in Iraq and Afghanistan, the deal is a testament to strong U.S.-Jordanian relations.

Economic Assistance

The United States provides economic aid to Jordan as both a cash transfer and for USAID programs in Jordan. The Jordanian government uses cash transfers to service its foreign debt.[60] Approximately 45% of Jordan's ESF allotment each year goes toward the cash transfer. USAID programs in Jordan focus on a variety of sectors including democracy assistance, water preservation, and education. In the democracy sector, U.S. assistance supports capacity building programs for the parliament's support offices, the Jordanian Judicial Council, Judicial Institute, and the Ministry of Justice. The International Republican Institute and the National Democratic Institute also receive U.S. grants to train, among other groups, some Jordanian political parties and members of parliament. In the water sector, the bulk of U.S. economic assistance is devoted to optimizing the management of scarce water resources, as Jordan is one of the most waterdeprived countries in the world. USAID is currently subsidizing several waste treatment and water distribution projects in the Jordanian cities of Amman, Aqaba, and Irbid.

The United States government also periodically assists Jordan with other forms of indirect economic aid. For example, in July 2008 the Overseas Private Investment Corporation signed a $250 million loan deal with three Jordanian banks to help them extend long-term mortgage lending to low-income citizens. These loans were in support of the king's plan to construct 100,000 houses over the next five years to help cash-strapped Jordanians.

Millennium Challenge Account (MCA)

In FY2006, Jordan was listed by the Millennium Challenge Corporation (MCC) as a Threshold country in the lower middle-income bracket. On September 12, 2006, the MCC's board of directors approved up to $25 million in Threshold Program assistance for Jordan. Even prior to the selection, the possible choice of Jordan had come under severe criticism. *Freedom House*, the organization whose annual Index of Freedom is drawn upon for two of the "Ruling Justly" indicators, urged the MCC board to bypass countries that had low scores on political rights and civil liberties. It argued that countries like Jordan that fall below 4 out of a possible 7 on its index should be automatically disqualified. Jordan, however, did well on three of the six other indicators in this category. Several development analysts further argued that Jordan should not be eligible, asserting that it is already one of the largest recipients of U.S. aid, has access to private sector capital, and is not a democracy. In selecting Jordan, the MCC board appears not to have been swayed by these arguments.

In September 2010, the Millennium Challenge Corporation approved a five-year, $275.1 million compact with the Hashemite Kingdom of Jordan to increase the supply of water available to households and businesses in the cities of Amman and Zarqa. The compact also will help improve the efficiency of water delivery, wastewater collection, and wastewater treatment. If estimates hold true, the clean drinking water generated as a result of the MCC compact may be enough to supply almost 1 million Jordanian citizens with freshwater.

Military Assistance

U.S. military assistance is primarily directed toward upgrading Jordan's air force, as recent purchases include upgrades to U.S.-made F-16 fighters, air-to-air missiles, and radar systems. FMF grants also provide financing for Jordan's purchase of U.S. Blackhawk helicopters in order to enhance Jordan's border monitoring and counter-terror capability. Jordan is currently the single largest provider of civilian police personnel and fifth-largest provider of military personnel to U.N. peacekeeping operations worldwide. In addition to large-scale military aid grants for conventional weapons purchases, Jordan also receives small grants of U.S. antiterrorism assistance from the Nonproliferation, Anti-Terrorism, Demining, and Related Programs account (NADR).[61]

Trade

Jordan ranked 78th among U.S. trading partners in volume of trade with the United States in 2010. According to the United States Trade Commission, in 2010 Jordan exported $973.8 million in goods and services to the United States, a large percentage of which consisted of apparel and clothing accessories. In 2010, Jordanian imports from the United States reached $1.13 billion. Principal U.S. commodities imported by Jordan consisted of aircraft parts, machinery and appliances, vehicles, and cereals. Two measures, in particular—the Free Trade Agreement and Qualifying Industrial Zones—have helped expand U.S.-Jordanian trade ties and could create more opportunities for U.S. investment in Jordan.

Free Trade Agreement

On October 24, 2000, then-President Clinton and King Abdullah II witnessed the signing of a U.S.-Jordanian Free Trade Agreement, which eliminated duties and commercial barriers to bilateral trade in goods and services originating in the two countries. Earlier, in a report released on September 26, 2000, the U.S. International Trade Commission concluded that a U.S.-Jordan Free Trade Agreement would have no measurable impact on total U.S. imports or exports, U.S. production, or U.S. employment. Under the agreement, the two countries agreed to enforce existing laws concerning worker rights and environmental protection. On January 6, 2001, then-President Clinton transmitted to the 107th Congress a proposal to implement the Free Trade Agreement. On July 23, then-U.S. Trade Representative Zoellick and then-Jordanian Ambassador Marwan Muasher exchanged letters pledging that the two sides would "make every effort" to resolve disputes without recourse to sanctions and other formal procedures. These letters were designed to allay concerns on the part of some Republican Members over the possible use of sanctions to enforce labor and environmental provisions of the treaty. President Bush signed H.R. 2603, which implemented the FTA as P.L. 107-43 on September 28, 2001, during King Abdullah's visit to Washington, DC, following the September 11, 2001, attacks.

Qualifying Industrial Zones

One outgrowth of the Jordanian-Israeli peace treaty was the establishment of "Qualifying Industrial Zones" (QIZs), under which goods produced with specified levels of Jordanian and Israeli input can enter the United States duty free, under the provisions of P.L. 104-234. This act amended previous legislation so as to grant the President authority to extend the U.S.-Israel free trade area to cover products from QIZs between Israel and Jordan or between Israel and Egypt. QIZs were designed both to help the Jordanian economy and to serve as a vehicle for expanding commercial ties between Jordan and Israel. Although QIZs have succeeded in boosting U.S.- Jordanian trade, there has been only a modest increase in Jordanian-Israeli trade.

Currently there are 13 QIZs in Jordan employing approximately 43,000 people (working eighthour days six days a week), 74% of whom are foreign workers from Southeast Asian nations including Pakistan, India, Bangladesh, and Sri Lanka. In general, foreign laborers are viewed as more skilled and productive than local Jordanians. In addition, it is difficult for employers to recruit local Jordanians since workers typically live on site, and many are hesitant to separate from their families, though in some areas local Jordanians are provided with free transportation to the QIZs. According to one Jordanian labor leader, foreign workers are attractive to employers because "they are like slaves. They work them day and night."[62] Labor rights activists also have complained that Jordanian workers in the QIZs are excluded from a new minimum wage law.

Sweat Shop Allegations

On May 3, 2006, the National Labor Committee (NLC), a New York-based human rights advocacy group, issued a report alleging sweatshop-like conditions in 28 out of 100 Qualified Industrial Zone (QIZ) plants in Jordan. The government subsequently acknowledged that it had failed in some instances to enforce its own labor laws and has taken action since to close down factories in violation of the law. The NLC has recognized the government's recent actions, though it has suggested that violations of worker rights may continue in smaller factories. Foreign companies with operations inside QIZs must provide food and housing for workers. Conditions in worker dormitories are reportedly inspected by retail garment buyers, and the government provides medical clinics and security for the zones.

In 2008, the Jordanian government signed an agreement with the International Labor Organization and International Finance Corporation to establish a voluntary monitoring program to check conditions in close to 100 apparel factories operating in the QIZs. According to Charles Kernaghan of the NLC, "a lot of people seem to be trying to get this thing straight, but in a country where you don't have a vibrant civil society and unions are not dealing with workers, and workers have virtually no voice, it is going to be problematic."

Table 1. Recent Foreign Military Sales to Jordan

Fiscal Year	Weapon System	$ Value of Sale	Prime Contractor
FY2006	National Command & Control System	$450 million	Northrop Grumman Corporation
FY2006	Black Hawk Helicopters	$60 million	Sikorsky Co. and General Electric
FY2006	Armored Personnel Carriers	$156 million	BAE Company
FY2008	Border Security System	$390 million	DRS Technologies Corp
FY2009	AMRAAM Missiles	$131 million	Raytheon
FY2009	Artillery Rocket Systems	$220 million	Multiple Companies
FY2010	Repair of F-16 Engines	$75 million	Pratt & Whitney
FY2010	JAVELIN Anti-Tank Guided Missiles	$388 million	Javelin Joint Venture

Source: Defense Security Cooperation Agency (DSCA).

Military Cooperation

Military Sales

The United States is helping Jordan to modernize its armed forces, which have been the traditional mainstay of the regime. The Jordanian military forces, though well trained and disciplined, are outnumbered and outgunned by each of Jordan's neighboring forces. In recent years, Jordan has used U.S. military assistance grants to purchase Advanced Medium Range Airto- Air Missiles, upgrades for its fleet of F-16 fighters (approximately 70-80), and Black Hawk helicopters. The United States also delivered three Patriot anti-missile batteries to Jordan in early 2003 prior to the start of U.S. military operations in Iraq.

Joint Exercises and Training

A U.S.-Jordanian Joint Military Commission has functioned since 1974. More than 300 Jordanian military personnel study in the United States each year. In recent years, Jordan is among the top three recipients of U.S. International Military Education and Training (IMET) funding. IMET also funds the equipping of English language labs in Jordan. Combined training exercises by U.S. and Jordanian military units continue to take place in Jordan (dubbed "Early Victor"), at least on an annual basis and sometimes more often. The above-mentioned courses conducted by Jordan for Iraqi military personnel are reportedly being funded by the United States under a program called the New Iraqi Army Training Project.[63] In addition, the United States has supported the construction of the King Abdullah II Center for Special Operations Training (KASOTC). The center, which has been partially financed by the United States including with $99 million in appropriations from the FY2005 Emergency Supplemental Act (P.L. 109-13), serves as a regional headquarters for counter-terrorism training.[64] In 2003, Jordan built a Special Operations Command and the Anti-Terrorism Center in order to boost counter-terrorism capabilities within the military.

Other Activities

Under the provisions of Section 517 of the Foreign Assistance Act of 1961 as amended, then- President Clinton designated Jordan as a major non-NATO ally of the United States, effective on November 13, 1996. According to a State Department spokesman, this status "makes Jordan eligible for priority consideration for transfer of excess defense articles, the use of already appropriated military assistance funds for procurement through commercial leases, the stockpiling of U.S. military material, and the purchase of depleted uranium munitions."

According to U.S. and Jordanian officials, Jordan has deployed two military hospitals to Afghanistan and Iraq, respectively, and has committed almost 600 health care professionals to the two facilities. Both facilities provide critical health care to numerous patients, including civilians. The hospital in Afghanistan cares for more than 650 patients a day, having treated more than 500,000 since it was first deployed in December 2001. In Iraq, Jordan helped train 50,000 policemen, helped the United States reach out to Sunni tribes and politicians in order to facilitate reconciliation, and still maintains a field hospital in Fallujah.

Jordan also regularly contributes peacekeeping forces to United Nations missions abroad.[65] In November 2006, a Jordanian United Nations peacekeeping patrol in the Haitian capital, Port-au- Prince, was killed while on patrol. Jordan has about 1,500 troops in the Brazilian-led U.N. force, which includes more than 8,000 soldiers and police supported by some 1,000 civilian personnel. Two other Jordanian soldiers were killed in January 2006. In 2009, five more Jordanian peacekeepers were killed in a plane crash during border surveillance mission while serving in Haiti. Three more Jordanian soldiers were killed during the devastating 2010 earthquake in Haiti.

Jordan's Role in Libya

In April 2011, an estimated six Jordanian Air Force fighter jets were deployed to the Mediterranean to participate in Operation Odyssey Dawn in order to provide logistical support for imposition of a no-fly zone over Libya and protect Jordanian military aircraft flying humanitarian aid to the Libyan people. In early April, Jordanian aircraft landed at Benghazi Airport with humanitarian supplies. Jordan has said it will not participate militarily in the NATO-led enforcement mission in Libya, but is willing to provide humanitarian aid if asked.

Jordan's Role in Afghanistan

Although the Jordanian government had publicly acknowledged a limited humanitarian presence in Afghanistan since major NATO operations began there in 2001, the December 30, 2009, terrorist attack against a CIA base in Khost, in which a Jordanian intelligence agent and royal family member was killed, shed light on Jordan's deeper cooperation against Al Qaeda and their Taliban allies.[66] Officially, Jordan has not acknowledged its intelligence role in Afghanistan. Numerous reports of joint CIA-GID cooperation have illustrated Jordan's long-standing, but unacknowledged cooperation with U.S. global counterterrorism. According to one unnamed U.S. source, "we have a close partnership with the Jordanians on counterterrorism matters. Having suffered serious losses from terrorist attacks on their own soil, they are keenly aware of the significant threat posed by extremists." Jordanian Prime Minister Samir al Rafa'i stated that "Being part of this world, we have to coordinate with other countries and exchange information about the location of terrorist groups. We will be everywhere as long as this is necessary for our national security." Some Jordanian Islamists have expressed dismay at the degree of Jordanian cooperation with the United States, and there is some concern that the 2009 incident might temper future U.S.-Jordanian intelligence cooperation.

In March 2010, NATO Secretary General Anders Fogh Rasmussen officially requested that Jordan play a role in training the Afghan Army. In response, Jordan has sent an unspecified number of instructors from its armed forces and security service to Afghanistan. Reportedly, Jordan has already trained 2,500 members of the Afghan special forces at the King Abdullah II Special Operations Training Centre.[67] Jordan also is helping to promote religious toleration by training Afghan imams.

In June 2011, a Jordanian Al Qaeda operative named Mahmoud Hamdan Nizal (aka Abu Dher al Urduni) was killed in a clash with U.S. troops in eastern Afghanistan. Nizal was from the city of Zarqa and was killed in a U.S. air or artillery strike.

Table 2. Annual U.S. Aid to Jordan Since the 1991 Gulf Crisis
($ in millions)

| Fiscal Year (FY) | Economic Assistance | | | Military Assistance | | Totals |
	Econ Spt	Food Devel	Peace Cp	FMF	IMET	
1991	35.0[a]	0	0	0	20.0a	1.3	56.30
1992	30.0[b]	20.0	0	0	20.0b	.6	70.60
1993[c]	5.0	30.0	0	0	9.0	.5	44.50
1994[d]	9.0	15.0	4.0	0	9.0	.8	37.80
1995	7.2	15.0	6.7	0	7.3	1.0	37.20
1996	7.2	21.0	7.9	0	200.0[e]	1.2	237.30
1997[f]	112.2	2.6	4.5	1.1	30.0	1.7	152.10
1998[f]	150.0	0	0	1.2	75.0[g]	1.6	227.80
1999	150.0	0	0	1.4	70.0[g]	1.6	223.00
1999 (Wye)	50.0	0	0	0	50.0	0	100.00
2000	150.0	0	0	1.7	75.0	1.6	228.30
2000 (Wye)	50.0	0	0	0	150.0	0	200.00[h]
2001	150.0	0	0	1.7	75.0	1.7	228.40
2002	150.0	0	0	1.6	75.0	2.0	228.60
2002 (Suppl.)	100.0	0	0	0	25.0	0	125.00
2003	250.0	0	0	1.0	198.0	2.4	451.40
2003 (Suppl.)	700.0	0	0	0	406.0	0	1,106.00
2004	250.0	0	0	2.3	206.0	2.9	461.20
2004 (Suppl.)	100.0	0	0	0	0	0	100.00
2005	250.0	0	0	1.6	206.0	3.0	460.60
2005 (Suppl.)	100.0	0	0	0	100.0	0	200.00
2006	247.5	0	0	1.6	207.9	3.0	460.00
2006 (Suppl.)	50.0	0	0	0	0	0	50.00
2007	245.0	0	0	0	206.0	3.1	454.10
2007 (Suppl.)	10.3	0	0	0	45.0	0	55.30i
2008	361.4	0	0	0	298.3	2.9	662.60
2008 (Suppl.)	200.0	0	0	0	50.0	0	250.00
2009	263.5	0	0	0	235.0 (150.0 in FY2010	3.1	501.60
2009 (Suppl.)	150.0	0	0	0	Advanced funding)	0	150.00
2010	363.0	0	0	0	300.0	3.8	666.8
2010 (Suppl.)	100.0	0	0	0	50.0	0	150.0
2011 (Estimate)	360.0	0	0	0	300.0	3.7	663.7
FY2012(Request)	360.0	0	0	0	300.0	3.7	663.7

Note: These figures do not include debt relief subsidy appropriations or small amounts for de-mining assistance and counter-terrorism assistance.

a. Suspended in April 1991 under P.L. 102-27; released in early 1993.

b. Released in late July 1993.

c. Restrictions on FY1993 funds waived by Presidential Determination (PD) 93-39, Sept. 17, 1993.

d. FY1994 funds released by PD 94-11, Jan. 13, 1994, waiving restrictions under P.L. 103-87.

e. Three components: $30 million (Administration's original request); $70 million in additional FMF under FY1996 appropriation (P.L. 104-134) to cover balance of F-16 aircraft package; and $100 million in special drawdown authority (P.L. 104-107).

f. These figures include $100 million in economic assistance under the President's Middle East Peace and Stability Fund ($100 million in FY1997, $116 million in FY1998).

g. For each of these two years, FMF figure includes $25 million in drawdown authority.

h. Some of these funds were obligated in later years (FY2001 or FY2002).

i. Total FY2007 supplemental aid to Jordan was $85.3 million. The above chart does not include $25 million in NADR funds.

End Notes

[1] Article 35 of Jordan's Constitution states that "The King appoints the Prime Minister and may dismiss him or accept his resignation. He appoints the Ministers; he also dismisses them or accepts their resignation, upon the recommendation of the Prime Minister."

[2] "Jordanian King's Mideast Outlook Dims," *Washington Post*, June 16, 2011.

[3] The committee recommends an election oversight panel consisting of 13 notable members, including seven retired judges appointed by a royal decree.

[4] The committee also increased seats allocated for women from 12 to 15.

[5] According to the proposal, voters would be able to vote for one list at the governorate level and one list at national level, both open lists where voters can choose three candidates.

[6] The U.S. Central Intelligence Agency estimates that official unemployment in 2010 reached 13.4%; according to the Agency, the "unofficial rate is approximately 30%." In December 2010, the IMF reported that "Jordan's economic recovery remains on track, on the back of slowly rising domestic activity. Fiscal prudence and credible monetary management, reinforced by strong supervision and regulation of the financial sector, provide a solid platform for a more robust upturn in 2011." International Monetary Fund (IMF), "Jordan—Aide-Mémoire for the 2010 Staff Visit Discussions," December 20, 2010.

[7] According to one report, "Electoral law reforms introduced in May 2010 have exacerbated tension between tribes in Jordan and led to widespread-but-contained tribal violence after the November parliamentary elections. The level of tribe-against-tribe violence in recent months, which occurred against a backdrop of rising tribal tension during the past few years, was unprecedented.... Smaller tribes feared that under the new electoral law, they would win fewer seats in parliament, limiting their ability to obtain pork barrel spending and state jobs." See, "Jordan: Potential for Tribal Violence Growing," Open Source Works, Central Intelligence Agency, Directorate of Intelligence, January 5, 2011.

[8] "The Revolt of Jordan's Military Veterans," *ForeignPolicy.com*, June 16, 2010.

[9] "Tribesmen in Jordan Issue Urgent Call for Political Reform," *New York Times*, February 7, 2011.

[10] Open Source Center, "Al-Jazirah: Tribes in Jordan Stage Protests, Demand Tribal Land," *Doha Al-Jazirah Satellite Channel Television in Arabic*, February 17, 2011, GMP 20110 217631001.

[11] "In Jordan, King Abdullah II Getting Earful from Tribal Leaders," *Los Angeles Times*, February 24, 2011.

[12] The December 2010 IMF report stated: "Further fiscal consolidation will be critical over the medium term to bring fiscal and external balances to a more comfortable level."

[13] The King also appointed independent Islamist Abdelrahim Akur as head of the Ministry of Islamic Affairs and Awqaf (endowments).

[14] See,http://www.washingtoninstitute.org/templateI05.php?&new ActiveSub Nav=PolicyWatch/ PeaceWatch&activeSubNavLink=templateI05. php%3F&new ActiveNav=analysis

[15] An array of youth-led protest groups have emerged in recent months, including *Jayin* (We are Coming) and April 15 youth. The Jordanian Muslim Brotherhood also has joined youth protestors, though some observers suggest that certain youth-led groups may not be comfortable in associating themselves with the agenda of the Muslim Brotherhood.

[16] The National Dialogue Committee is expected to release its reform recommendations in June 2011. It is expected to address laws on the formation of political parties and elections, but few experts expect it to propose other constitutional amendments that would limit the King's power in any meaningful way.

[17] The amendment has passed the Lower Assembly of parliament but not the royally-appointed Senate.

[18] "Uneasy Balancing Act in Jordan," *New York Times*, April 13, 2011.

[19] Over 80 percent of the government's budget is allocated for civil service salaries and military pensions. For 2011, Jordan's budget deficit is projected to be $1.7 billion. Total Jordanian domestic ($9.3 billion) and foreign debt ($6.3 billion) is $15.6 billion or 57.8% of annual GDP. Jordan's public debt law sets the debt ceiling at 60 percent of GDP.

[20] Nathan J. Brown, *Jordan: Not on the Brink but in Crisis*, Carnegie Endowment for International Peace, February 22, 2011.

[21] Speculation over the ratio of East Bankers to Palestinians (those who arrived as refugees and immigrants since 1948) in Jordanian society tends to be a sensitive domestic issue. Jordan last conducted a national census in 2004, and it is unclear whether or not the government maintains such statistics. Over time, intermarriage has made it more difficult to discern distinct differences between the two communities, though divisions do persist.

[22] In July 2009, King Abdullah II named his 15-year-old son, Prince Hussein Bin Abdullah, as crown prince. The position had been vacant since 2004, when King Abdullah II removed the title from his half-brother, Prince Hamzah.

[23] During the late 1970s and early 1980s, the parliament was suspended and legislative powers reverted to the government.

[24] The king also is allowed to declare martial law and suspend the provisions of the constitution. See United Nations Development Program (UNDP), Programme on Governance in the Arab Region (POGAR), Historical Background of Jordan's Constitution, available online at http://www.undp-pogar.org/countries/constitution.asp?cid=7.

[25] According to one expert, "When parliament was out of session between 2001 and 2003, over 200 provisional laws were passed, many of them containing controversial economic reform provisions. Similarly, since November 2009, when the parliament was dismissed a second time, the Samir Rifai government has ushered through more than thirty provisional laws dealing with contentious issues like pensions, taxes, utilities pricing, and -- of course – electoral reform." See, "Jordan: Just What Exactly Are We Promoting?" *Foreign Policy. Com*, October 12, 2010.

[26] CRS interview with Jordanian lawmakers, May 2006.

[27] The 1993 law was adopted during a period when parliament was suspended. It has never received the formal approval of parliament, raising questions over its constitutional legitimacy.

[28] Under Jordan's system, electoral districts return several members to parliament, but a voter may vote for only one candidate. Seats are then awarded to as many of the highest-polling individual candidates as there are seats allocated to that district.

[29] According to one study of Jordan's election law, "It is no coincidence that under-represented urban governorates have a large population of Palestinian origin, and that over-represented largely rural governorates are considered mainstays of support for the regime." See, David M. DeBartolo, "Jordan: Attention Turns to Electoral Law," *Arab Reform Bulletin*, published by the Carnegie Endowment for International Peae, Volume 5, Issue 3, April 2007. In Amman, each legislator represents about 95,000 people. In certain rural provinces, a legislator represents as few as 2,000 individuals.

[30] See, Dima Toukan Tabbaa, "Jordan's New Electoral Law Disappoints Reformers," *Arab Reform Bulletin*, June 22, 2010.

[31] Jillian Schwedler, "Jordan's Risky Business As Usual," *Middle East Report Online*, June 30, 2010.

[32] "Jordan's New Electoral Law and Its Implications," *ForeignPolicy.com*, May 24, 2010.

[33] See, Press Statement, Philip J. Crowley, Assistant Secretary, Bureau of Public Affairs, November 10, 2010.

[34] Jordan possesses substantial reserves of phosphates and potash. No significant oil and gas fields have been discovered. However, Jordan has one of world's largest reserves of oil shale. Officials estimate that the country contains the world's fourth-largest oil shale reserves. In 2006, Shell signed an oil shale exploration agreement with the Jordanian government. Estonia's Eesti Energia AS also has signed agreements on oil shale projects. See, "Amman Unlocks Energy Potential," *Middle East Economic Digest*, August 7, 2009.

[35] It is estimated that up to 20% of GDP comes from remittances. Nearly 10% of Jordan's population (600,000 est.) reside and work in Arab Gulf countries.

[36] One factor that exacerbates the unemployment situation in Jordan is the social stigma attached to menial labor jobs. Referred to as the "culture of shame," Jordanian tribal traditions look down on certain types of employment such as construction. In fact, the government estimates that there are approximately 300,000 to 400,000 foreign laborers in Jordan working as domestic laborers, bricklayers, and other tasks.

[37] Jordan was ranked 49 out of 180 countries surveyed in Transparency International's 2009 Corruption Perceptions Index.

[38] Jordan accounts for 2% of the world's uranium reserves.

[39] According to various Jordanian reports, Jordan will contribute $60 million toward the overall cost of the reactor with the rest made up by a South Korean government loan.

[40] Open Source Center, "Israeli Officials Fear Jordanian Nuclear Plant on Earthquake-Prone Dead Sea Rift," *Yedi'ot Aharonot (in Hebrew)*, October 1, 2009, Document ID# GMP 20091001735011.

[41] CRS Report R40344, *The United Arab Emirates Nuclear Program and Proposed U.S. Nuclear Cooperation*, by Christopher M. Blanchard and Paul K. Kerr.

[42] Open Source Center, "Jordan Atomic Energy Official Cited on Nuclear Program; Fear of US 'Terms' Noted," *Al Jazirah.net*, April 1, 2010, GMP20100402676001.

[43] "Jordan and U.S. Move Closer to Nuclear Pact," *Wall Street Journal*, February 10, 2010.

[44] "Jordan's Nuclear Ambitions Pose Quandary for the U.S. ," *Wall Street Journal*, June 15, 2010.

[45] U.S. Department of State, "Remarks With Jordanian Foreign Minister Nasser Judeh," Hillary Rodham Clinton, Secretary of State, Marka Airbase, Amman, Jordan, September 16, 2010.

[46] "Jordan Sees Nuclear Accord with U.S. by Year-End," *Reuters*, September 28, 2010.

[47] In 1991, Congress suspended the delivery of U.S. economic and military aid to Jordan. See Section 502 of P.L. 102- 27, the Dire Emergency Supplemental Appropriations for Consequences of Operation Desert Shield/Desert Storm, Food Stamps, Unemployment Compensation Administration, Veterans Compensation and Pensions, and Urgent Needs for the Fiscal Year Ending September 30, 1991 and For Other Purposes.

[48] Jordan and Israel signed a peace treaty on October 26, 1994. Later, the two countries exchanged ambassadors; Israel returned approximately 131 square miles of territory near the Rift Valley to Jordan; the parliament repealed laws banning contacts with Israel; and the two countries signed a number of bilateral agreements between 1994 and 1996 to normalize economic and cultural links. Water sharing, a recurring problem, was partially resolved in May 1997 when the two countries reached an interim arrangement under which Israel began pumping 72,000 cubic meters of water from Lake Tiberias (the Sea of Galilee) to Jordan per day (equivalent to 26.3 million cubic meters per year—a little over half the target amount envisioned in an annex to the peace treaty).

[49] The United Nations Relief and Works Agency for Palestine Refugees in the Near East (UNRWA) maintains a large presence in Jordan. UNRWA has 7,000 staff in Jordan, comprising mostly teachers, doctors, and engineers. It operates 174 schools in Jordan (providing education through 10th grade, then the remainder provided by government). According to UNRWA officials, their budget is $104 million a year. At this point, 83% of all U.N.-registered refugees live outside of UNRWA camps.

[50] In 1997, Israeli agents disguised as Canadian tourists attempted to poison Khaled Meshaal, head of the Hamas political bureau and one of its founding members. The agents were captured by Jordanian authorities, and Israel was forced to release a number of high profile Hamas members in order to secure the return of their operatives. King Hussein had reportedly threatened to abrogate the Israel-Jordan 1994 peace treaty if Israel failed to provide an antidote and release other Hamas prisoners.

[51] "Palestinian Forces Enter Jordan for Training Under U.S. Program," *Ha'aretz*, January 24, 2008 and "500 Palestinian Security Force Members Head to Jordan for U.S.-funded Training," *Ha'aretz*, September 18, 2008. Jordan has helped train 3,000 Palestinian cadets at the U.S.-funded Jordan International Police Training Center (JIPTC).

[52] "Report on Jordan-Hamas Talks," *Al-Hayat* (London), accessed via Open Source Center, Document ID# GMP20080817837001, August 17, 2008.

[53] "Egypt and Jordan Quietly Back Abbas, Too," *Christian Science Monitor*, June 20, 2007.

[54] For years, some experts have speculated that Central Intelligence Agency (CIA) support to the GID has been substantial. One expert wrote that "the agency created a Jordanian intelligence service, which lives today as its liaison to much of the Arab world." See, Tim Weiner, *Legacy of Ashes*, New York, Anchor Books, 2008. In addition, there is a long history of U.S.-Jordanian intelligence cooperation. According to *Jane's Intelligence Digest*, the GID collaborated with the U.S. Central Intelligence Agency in the early 1980s to disrupt the Abu Nidal organization and in 1999 was instrumental in foiling Al-Qaeda's 'millennium plot.' It also may have been responsible for foiling planned bombings of the US, Jordanian and British embassies in Beirut in 2001 as well as the US embassy in Amman in 2004. See, "Jordanian-US intelligence co-operation: Iraq and beyond," *Jane's Intelligence Digest*, November 9, 2007.

[55] "Typical of a New Terror Threat: Anger of a Gunman in Jordan," *New York Times*, September 6, 2006.

[56] "Jordan's Spy Agency: Holding Cell for the CIA," *Washington Post*, December 1, 2007.

[57] "Group: Jordan Tortures Suspects for U.S.," *Associated Press*, July 24, 2006.

[58] "Jordan: Torture in Prisons Routine and Widespread," *Human Rights Watch*, October 8, 2008.

[59] Under the terms of the MOU, annual foreign aid (non-supplemental) to Jordan will rise by nearly 50%, from an estimated $460 million per year to $660 million.

[60] When providing cash transfer assistance, the United States, though USAID, requires the Jordanian government to meet certain mutually-agreed upon benchmarks. According to USAID, these benchmarks include, among others, the Government of Jordan approving an Insolvency and Bankruptcy draft law, streamlining the consultation process required for registering property, approving a Medical Liability draft law, approving the Anti-Money Laundering Unit (AMLU) By-Laws, amending the Judicial Independence Law to allow for the formation of a Judges Association, and allowing Iraqis returning home to exit the

Kingdom without paying overstay fees or incurring a bar to reentry. CRS Correspondence with USAID, March 3, 2011.

[61] Since FY2002, Jordan has received an annual average of approximately $2 million in NADR appropriations from Congress. NADR funds helps train civilian security and law enforcement personnel from friendly governments in police procedures that deal with terrorism.

[62] "Industrial Zones Create Little Work for Jordanians," *Financial Times*, February 9, 2009.

[63] Riad Kahwaji, "Forging a New Iraqi Army—in Jordan," *Defense News*, February 9, 2004, p. 8.

[64] According to one description of the new U.S.-Jordanian facility, "If special forces have to conduct house-to-house searches, KASOTC provides that infrastructure in a training environment.... If they have to rescue hostages on an airplane, KASOTC provides the plane. If they have to rescue hostages from an embassy, KASOTC provides an embassy structure." See, Joan Kibler, "KASOTC," *Special Operations Technology Online Edition*, volume 6, issue 2, March 19, 2008.

[65] To date, the Jordanian Armed Forces (JAF) have contributed 57,000 troops to 18 different United Nations peacekeeping missions.

[66] On December 30, 2009, Humam Khalil Abu Mulal al Balawi, a Jordanian terrorist who had been serving as an informant for the Central Intelligence Agency and Jordan's General Intelligence Directorate, detonated a suicide vest bomb killing eight people outside CIA Forward Operating Base Chapman in Khost, Afghanistan. His Jordanian handler, Captain Sharif Ali bin Zeid, a member of the royal family, was killed as well. Al Balawi, a physician, held virulent anti-American and anti-Israeli views expressed in various Jihadist online forums. Prior to his attack, he had managed to convince U.S. and Jordanian intelligence officials that he knew the whereabouts of Ayman Al Zawahiri, who is Al Qaeda's second-in-command. In a video filmed before his death, Al Balawi swore revenge for the August 2009 killing of Pakistani Taliban leader Baitullah Mehsud and appeared with Mehsud's cousin and successor Hakimullah Mehsud. Months later, a second video emerged showing Al Balawi urging militants to target Jordan for terrorist attacks.

[67] "Jordan Trained 2,500 Afghan Special Forces: Minister," *Agence France Presse*, May 12, 2010.

In: Bahrain and Jordan   ISBN: 978-1-61942-605-4
Editors: K. Buck and T. J. McPherson   © 2012 Nova Science Publishers, Inc.

Chapter 3

BAHRAIN COUNTRY PROFILE[*]

United States Department of State

Official Name: Kingdom of Bahrain

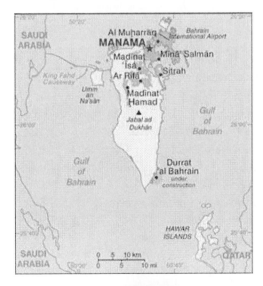

Flag of Bahrain.

---

[*] This is an edited, reformatted and augmented version of a Bureau of Near Eastern Affairs
Profile, dated January 13, 2012.

GEOGRAPHY

Area: 727 sq. km. (274 sq. mi.); approximately four times the size of Washington, DC. Bahrain is an archipelago of 36 islands located off the eastern coast of Saudi Arabia. The four main islands are joined by causeways, and make up about 95% of the total land area. Cities:
Capital: Manama (pop. 148,000; 2002 est.). *Other cities*--Al Muharraq.
Terrain: Low desert plain (highest elevation point--122 m).
Climate: Hot and humid from May-September, with average highs ranging from 30°-40° C (86°-104° F). Maximum temperatures average 20°-30° C (68°-86° F) the remainder of the year.

PEOPLE

Nationality: *Noun and adjective*--Bahraini(s).
Population (2010): 1,214,705, including about 235,108 non-nationals. Annual population growth rate (2009): 2%.
Ethnic groups: Bahraini 63%, Asian 19%, other Arab 10%, Iranian 8%.
Religions: 98% Muslim (approximately Shi'a 70%, Sunni 30%), with small Christian, Jewish, Baha'i, and Hindu communities.
Languages: Arabic (official), English, Farsi, and Urdu are also widely spoken.
Education: Education is not compulsory, but is provided free to Bahrainis and non-nationals at all levels, including higher education. *Estimated net primary school attendance* (2008)--97.8%. *Adult literacy, age 15 and over* (2008)--90.8% for the overall population (male 91.9%, female 89.4%).
Health: *Infant mortality rate* (2009)--9.5 deaths/1,000 live births. *Life expectancy*--76 yrs. males, 80 yrs. females.
Work force (2006 est.): 352,000 of which 44% were foreigners.

GOVERNMENT

Type: Constitutional hereditary monarchy.
Independence: August 15, 1971 (from the United Kingdom).
Constitution: Approved and promulgated May 26, 1973; suspended on August 26, 1975; the National Action Charter was approved by a national

popular referendum on February 14-15, 2001, and a new constitution was issued on February 14, 2002.

Branches: *Executive*--King (chief of state); Prime Minister (head of government); Council of Ministers (cabinet) is appointed by the King and headed by the Prime Minister.

Legislative--The bicameral parliament (al-Majlis al-Watani) consists of a 40-member elected Council of Representatives and a 40-member Shura (Consultative) Council appointed by the King. Members of both chambers serve 4-year terms.

Judicial--High Civil Appeals Court. The judiciary is independent with right of judicial review.

Administrative subdivisions: 12 municipalities (manatiq): Al Hidd, Al Manamah, Al Mintaqah al Gharbiyah, Al Mintaqah al Wusta, Al Mintaqah ash Shamaliyah, Al Muharraq, Ar Rifa' wa al Mintaqah al Janubiyah, Jidd Hafs, Madinat Hamad, Madinat 'Isa, Juzur Hawar, Sitrah. Suffrage: Universal at age 18.

ECONOMY

GDP (2009): $20.59 billion.

Real GDP growth rate (2010): 4.5%.

Per capita GDP (2009 est.): $38,400.

Natural resources: Oil, aluminum, textiles, natural gas, fish, pearls.

Agriculture (less than 1% of GDP): *Products*--fruit, vegetables, poultry, dairy products, shrimp, fish.

Industry: *Types*--oil and gas (10% of GDP), manufacturing (12.4% of GDP), aluminum.

Services: Finance (30% of GDP), transport and communications (8.9% of GDP), real estate (9.2% of GDP), government services (14.8% of GDP).

Trade (2009 est.): *Exports*--$12.5 billion: oil and other mineral products, aluminum, textiles. *Major markets*--Saudi Arabia (3.4%), U.S. (3%), India (2.7%), Japan (2.3%). *Imports*--$10.37 billion: crude oil, machinery and appliances, transport equipment, foodstuffs. *Major suppliers*--Saudi Arabia (26.7%), Japan (8.9%), U.S. (7.8%), China (6.2%), Germany (4.8%), South Korea (4.7%), U.A.E. (4.2%).

PEOPLE

Bahrain is one of the most densely populated countries in the world; about 89% of the population lives in the two principal cities of Manama and Al Muharraq. Approximately 66% of the indigenous population is originally from the Arabian Peninsula and Iran. Bahrain has a sizeable foreign labor force. The government's policies on naturalization remain controversial. In June 2002, the King issued a decree allowing citizens of the Gulf Cooperation Council (GCC) to take up dual Bahraini nationality. Opposition political groups charge that the government is granting citizenship to foreign nationals who have served in the Bahraini armed forces and security services to alter the demographic balance of the country, which is primarily Shi'a. According to passport officials, about 40,000 individuals have been naturalized over the past 50 years (about 10% of the total population).

The indigenous population is 98% Muslim. Although some two-thirds of the indigenous population is Shi'a Muslim, the ruling family and the majority of government, military, and corporate leaders are Sunni Muslims. The small indigenous Christian and Jewish communities make up the remaining 2% of the population. Roughly half of foreign resident community are non-Muslim, and include Christians, Hindus, Baha'is, Buddhists and Sikhs.

Bahrain has invested its oil revenues in developing an advanced educational system. The first public schools for girls and boys were opened in the 1920s. The government continues to pay for all schooling costs. Although school attendance is not compulsory, primary and secondary attendance rates are high, and literacy rates are currently among the highest in the region. Higher education is available for secondary school graduates at the Bahrain University, Arabian Gulf University and specialized institutes including the College of Health Sciences--operating under the direction of the Ministry of Health--which trains physicians, nurses, pharmacists, and paramedics. The government has identified providing educational services to the Gulf Cooperation Council as a potential economic growth area, and is actively working to establish Bahrain as a regional center for higher education.

HISTORY

The site of the ancient Bronze Age civilization of Dilmun, Bahrain was an important center linking trade routes between Mesopotamia and the Indus Valley as early as 5,000 years ago. The Dilmun civilization began to decline about 2,000 B.C. as trade from India was cut off. From 750 B.C. on, Assyrian kings repeatedly claimed sovereignty over the islands. Shortly after 600 B.C., Dilmun was formally incorporated into the new Babylonian empire. There are no historical references to Bahrain until Alexander the Great's arrival in the Gulf in the 4th century B.C. Although Bahrain was ruled variously by the Arab tribes of Bani Wa'el and Persian governors, Bahrain continued to be known by its Greek name Tylos until the 7th century, when many of its inhabitants converted to Islam. A regional pearling and trade center, Bahrain came under the control of the Ummayad Caliphs of Syria, the Abbasid Caliphs of Baghdad, Persian, Omani and Portuguese forces at various times from the 7th century until the Al Khalifa family, a branch of the Bani Utbah tribe that have ruled Bahrain since the 18th century, succeeded in capturing Bahrain from a Persian garrison controlling the islands in 1783.

In the 1830s the Al Khalifa family signed the first of many treaties establishing Bahrain as a British Protectorate. Similar to the binding treaties of protection entered into by other Persian Gulf principalities, the agreements entered into by the Al Khalifas prohibited them from disposing of territory and entering into relationships with any foreign government without British consent in exchange for British protection against the threat of military attack from Ottoman Turkey. The main British naval base in the region was moved to Bahrain in 1935 shortly after the start of large-scale oil production.

In 1968, when the British Government announced its decision (reaffirmed in March 1971) to end the treaty relationships with the Persian Gulf sheikdoms, Bahrain initially joined the other eight states (Qatar and the seven Trucial Sheikhdoms now the United Arab Emirates) under British protection in an effort to form a union of Arab emirates. The nine sheikhdoms still had not agreed on terms of union by 1971, however, prompting Bahrain to declare itself fully independent on August 15, 1971.

Bahrain promulgated a constitution and elected its first parliament in 1973, but just 2 years later, in August 1975, the Amir disbanded the National Assembly after it attempted to legislate the end of Al-Khalifa rule and the expulsion of the U.S. Navy from Bahrain. In the 1990s, Bahrain suffered from repeated incidents of political violence stemming from the disaffection of the Shi'a majority. In response, the Amir instituted the first Bahraini cabinet change in 20 years in 1995 and also increased the membership of the Consultative Council, which he had created in 1993 to provide advice and opinion on legislation proposed by the cabinet and, in certain cases, suggest new laws on its own, from 30 to 40 the following year. These steps led to an initial decline in violent incidents, but in early 1996 a number of hotels and restaurants were bombed, resulting in several fatalities. Over 1,000 people were arrested and held in detention without trial in connection with these disturbances. The government has since released these individuals (see Government and Political Conditions Section below for details).

GOVERNMENT AND POLITICAL CONDITIONS

Shaikh Hamad bin Isa Al Khalifa acceded to the throne in March 1999, after the death of his father Shaikh Isa bin Hamad Al Khalifa, Bahrain's ruler since 1961. He championed a program of democratic reform shortly after his accession. In November 2000, Shaikh Hamad established a committee to create a blueprint to transform Bahrain from a hereditary emirate to a constitutional monarchy within 2 years. The resulting "National Action Charter" was presented to the Bahraini public in a referendum in February 2001. In the first comprehensive public vote in Bahrain since the 1970s, 94.8% of voters overwhelmingly endorsed the charter. That same month, Shaikh Hamad pardoned all political prisoners and detainees, including those who had been imprisoned, exiled or detained on security charges. He also abolished the State Security Law and the State Security Court, which had permitted the government to detain individuals without trial for up to 3 years.

On February 14, 2002, 1 year after the referendum endorsing his National Action Charter, Shaikh Hamad pronounced Bahrain a constitutional monarchy and changed his status from Amir to King. He simultaneously announced that the first municipal elections since 1957 would be held in May 2002, and that a bicameral parliament, with a representative lower house, would be reconstituted with parliamentary elections in October 2002. As part of these constitutional reforms, the government created an independent financial watchdog empowered to investigate cases of embezzlement and violations of state expenditure in July 2002.

Turnout for the May 2002 municipal elections was 51%, with female voters making up 52% of voters. Turnout for the 2002 parliamentary elections--the first in almost 3 decades--was 53% in the first round and 43% in the second round, despite the fact that four political societies, including the largest Shi'a society, organized a boycott to protest constitutional provisions enacted by the King that gave the appointed upper chamber of parliament voting rights equal to the elected lower chamber. The new parliament held its first joint sitting in December 2002. Bahrain held its second set of parliamentary and municipal elections in November and December 2006. All registered political societies participated in the elections and a Shi'a society, Al Wifaq, represented the largest single bloc inside the Council of Representatives. Thirty-two of the Council's 40 members represented Sunni and Shi'a Islamist societies. One woman, Lateefah Al-Qauod, ran uncontested and became the first woman elected to parliament in Bahrain. Parliamentary and municipal elections were held again in 2010.

In February and March 2011, Bahrain experienced a period of civil unrest inspired in part by recent revolutions in Egypt and Tunisia and in part by local dissatisfaction with government policies. Bahraini security forces moved quickly to restore order. Bahrain hosted military forces from Saudi Arabia, U.A.E., and Kuwait under the aegis of the GCC Peninsula Shield Force to secure critical infrastructure while Bahraini security forces contained unrest. An ongoing National Dialogue seeks to address political grievances between political societies, civil society groups, and the government to prevent further instances of unrest.

Bahrain has a complex system of courts, based on diverse legal sources, including Sunni and Shi'a Sharia (religious law), tribal law, and other civil codes and regulations created with the help of British advisers in the early 20th century. In 2001, Shaikh Hamad created the Supreme Judicial Council to regulate these courts and separate the administrative and judicial branches of government.

Principal Government Officials

King--Hamad bin Isa Al Khalifa
Crown Prince and Commander in Chief of the Bahrain
Defense Force--Salman bin Hamad bin Isa Al Khalifa
Prime Minister--Khalifa bin Salman Al Khalifa
Deputy Premier--Jawad bin Salem Al Arrayed Deputy
Premier--Mohammad bin Mubarak Al Khalifa
Deputy Premier--Ali bin Khalifa Al Khalifa
Foreign Minister--Khalid bin Ahmed Al Khalifa
Ambassador to the United States--Houda Nonoo
Ambassador to the United Nations--Tawfeeq Al-Ahmed Al-Mansoor

Bahrain maintains an embassy in the United States at 3502 International Drive NW, Washington, DC 20008; tel: [1] (202) 342-1111; fax: [1] (202) 362-2192. The Bahraini Mission to the UN is located at 866 Second Avenue, New York, NY 10017; tel: [1] (212)223-6200; fax [1] (212) 319-0687.

Economy

The first Gulf state to discover oil, Bahrain's reserves are expected to run out in 10-15 years. Accordingly, Bahrain has worked to diversify its economy over the past decade and has stabilized its oil production at about 40,000 barrels per day (b/d). Revenues from oil and natural gas currently account for approximately 10% of GDP yet currently provide about 75% of government income. The state-owned Bahrain Petroleum Company refinery built in 1935, the first in the Gulf, has a capacity of about 260,000 b/d. Saudi Arabia provides most of the crude for refinery operation via pipeline. Through an agreement with Saudi Arabia, Bahrain also receives half of the net output and revenues from Saudi Arabia's Abu Saafa offshore oilfield.

The Bahrain National Gas Company operates a gas liquefaction plant that utilizes gas piped directly from Bahrain's oilfields. Gas reserves should last about 50 years at present rates of consumption. However, rising domestic demand spurred by a recent development boom has highlighted the need to increase gas supplies. The Gulf Petrochemical Industries Company is a joint venture of the petrochemical industries of Kuwait, the Saudi Basic Industries Corporation, and the Government of Bahrain. The plant, completed in 1985, produces ammonia and methanol for export. Growth in the hydrocarbons sector will be contingent upon new discoveries--Bahrain awarded exploration rights to Malaysia's Petronas and the U.S.'s Chevron Texaco after the resolution of Bahrain's long-standing territorial dispute with Qatar, but no meaningful finds have been announced to date. Bahrain's other industries include the majority state-owned Aluminum Bahrain (Alba)--which operates the largest aluminum smelter in the world outside Eastern Europe with an annual production of about 843,000 metric tons (mt) in 2005 after the completion of an expansion program--and related factories, such as the Aluminum Extrusion Company and the Gulf Aluminum Rolling Mill. Other plants include the Arab Iron and Steel Company's iron ore pelletizing plant (4 million tons annually) and a shipbuilding and repair yard.

Bahrain's development as a major financial center has been the most widely heralded aspect of its diversification effort. Bahrain is a regional financial and business center; international financial institutions operate in Bahrain, both offshore and onshore, without impediments, and the financial sector is currently the largest contributor to GDP at 30%. Over 370 offshore banking units and representative offices are located in Bahrain, as well as 65 American firms. Bahrain has also made a concerted effort to become the leading Islamic finance center in the Arab world, standardizing regulations of the Islamic banking industry. It currently has 32 Islamic commercial, investment and leasing banks as well as Islamic insurance (takaful) companies--the largest concentration of Islamic financial institutions in the Middle East.

Bahrain is working to develop other service industries such as information technology, healthcare, and education. The government has used its oil revenues to build an advanced infrastructure in transportation and telecommunications. The state monopoly--Batelco--was broken in April 2003 following the establishment of the Telecommunications Regulatory Authority (TRA). Since that time, the TRA has granted some 63 licenses in the interest of promoting healthy industry competition.

Bahrain plans to expand its airport, one of the busiest in the Gulf. More than 4.8 million passengers transited Bahrain International Airport in 2005. A modern, busy port offers direct and frequent cargo shipping connections to the U.S., Europe, and the Far East. To boost its competitiveness as a regional center, Bahrain is building a new port and has privatized port operations.

The government of Bahrain moved toward privatizing the production of electricity and water by licensing Al Ezzal to construct an independent power plant at a cost of $500 million. The company commenced operations in May 2006. In January 2006, the government announced the sale of the Al Hidd Power Plant for $738 million to Hidd Power Company, a consortium of British, Japanese, and Belgian companies.

Regional tourism is also a significant source of income. The government continues to favor large-scale tourism projects. It opened the only Formula One race track in the Middle East in 2004, and has awarded tenders for several tourist complexes. New hotel and spa projects are progressing within the context of broader real estate development, much of which is geared toward attracting increased tourism.

Government revenues continue to be largely dependent on the oil industry. Bahrain has received significant budgetary support and project grants from Saudi Arabia, Kuwait, and the United Arab Emirates. Buoyed by rising oil revenues, the 2007-2008 budget approved by the parliament in July 2006 provided for sizable increases in urban development, education, and social spending. Ministry of Defense spending was expected to account for 13% of current spending in 2007 and 2008 based on the new budget. The Ministry of Education and Ministry of the Interior also received substantial budget allocations. Significant capital outlays were allocated to improving housing and infrastructure in line with government efforts to raise the standard of living of the Shi'a population and to attract foreign investment.

The government has also started to extend protections to workers. Private sector employees won permission to form unions in late 2002; King Hamad has given his tentative approval for the formation of unions in government departments. In June 2006, Bahrain passed laws legalizing the existence of multiple trade federations and codifying several protections for workers engaged in union activity. As part of the government's labor reform program, it has formed a Labor Market Regulatory Authority and established a fund to support the training of Bahraini workers.

In 2006, bilateral trade exceeded $1 billion for the first time, representing almost 50% growth over 2005. The U.S.-Bahrain Free Trade Agreement took effect on August 1, 2006 and is generating increased U.S. commercial interest in Bahrain.

DEFENSE

The Bahrain Defense Force (BDF) numbers about 12,000 personnel and consists of army, navy, air force, air defense, and royal guard units. The public security forces and the coast guard are separate from the BDF and report to the Ministry of the Interior. Bahrain also has a national guard that consists of about 1,200 personnel. Bahrain's defense spending since 1999 has been steady. The government spends around $630 million annually on the military, about 20% of current expenditures. The parliamentary process has produced spirited debate over government spending, particularly defense spending, but no actual reductions.

With the help of the U.S. and the Gulf Cooperation Council, Bahrain has made significant efforts to upgrade its defense systems and modernize its armed forces over the last 20 years. In 1982, the GCC gave Bahrain $1.7 billion for this purpose. Since the 1991 Gulf War, the U.S. has provided military and defense technical assistance and training to Bahrain from Foreign Military Sales (FMS), commercial sources, and excess defense article sales

(EDA), and under the International Military and Education Training (IMET) program. The U.S. Office of Military Cooperation in Bahrain is attached to the U.S. Embassy and manages the security assistance mission. U.S. military sales to Bahrain since 2000 total $1.4 billion. Principal U.S. military systems acquired by the BDF include eight Apache helicopters, 54 M60A3 tanks, 22 F-16C/D aircraft, 51 Cobra helicopters, 9 MLRS Launchers (with ATACMS), 20 M109A5 Howitzers, 1 Avenger AD system, and the TPS-59 radar system. Bahrain has received $195 million in FMF and $410 million in U.S. EDA acquisition value delivered since the U.S.-Bahraini program began in 1993. The Bahrain Defense Force also placed orders for 9 UH-60M Blackhawk helicopters and 2 Mk-V Fast Patrol Boats. Delivery of both systems was planned for 2009.

Military exercises are conducted on a regular basis to increase the BDF's readiness and improve coordination with the U.S. and other GCC forces. The BDF also sends personnel to the United States for military training. This training includes courses from graduate-level professional military education down to entry-level technical training.

FOREIGN RELATIONS

Since achieving independence in 1971, Bahrain has pursued a policy of close consultation with neighboring states. Bahrain became a member of the United Nations and the Arab League in 1971. In 1981 it joined its five neighbors--Saudi Arabia, Oman, Kuwait, the U.A.E., and Qatar--to form the strategic Gulf Cooperation Council (GCC). Bahrain has complied with GCC efforts to coordinate economic development and defense and security planning. In December 1994, for example, Bahrain concurred with the GCC decision to drop secondary and tertiary boycotts against Israel. Bahrain also responded positively to Kuwait's request to deploy the GCC collective defense Peninsula Shield Force during the buildup and execution of Operation Iraqi Freedom (OIF) in 2003.

In addition to maintaining strong relations with its largest financial backers, Saudi Arabia, Kuwait, and the U.A.E., Bahrain has worked to improve its relations with Qatar and has proper, but not warm, relations with Iran. Bahrain-Iran relations have been strained since the discovery in 1981 of an Iran-sponsored coup plot in Bahrain. Bahraini suspicions of the Iranian role in local unrest in the mid-1990s remain. On March 16, 2001, the International Court of Justice (ICJ) announced its judgment on the long-standing maritime delimitation and territorial dispute between Bahrain and Qatar. The binding judgment awarded sovereignty over the Hawar Islands and Qit'at Jaradah to Bahrain and sovereignty over Zubarah (part of the Qatar Peninsula), Janan Island, and Fasht ad Dibal to Qatar. The peaceful settlement of this dispute has allowed for renewed co-operation, including plans to construct a causeway between the two countries.

Bahrain's strategic partnership with the U.S. has intensified since 1991. Bahraini pilots flew strikes in Iraq during the 1991 Gulf War, and the country was used as a base for military operations in the Gulf. Bahrain provided logistical and basing support to international maritime interdiction efforts to enforce UN sanctions and prevent illegal smuggling of oil from Iraq in the 1990s. Bahrain also provided extensive basing and overflight clearances for a multitude of U.S. aircraft operating in support of Operation Enduring Freedom (OEF) and Operation Iraqi Freedom (OIF). Bahrain deployed forces in support of coalition operations during both OEF and OIF. Bahrain has delivered humanitarian support and technical training to support the reconstruction of the Iraqi banking sector, and has offered support for each stage of Iraq's political transformation. Bahrain has also cooperated effectively on criminal investigation issues in support of efforts against terrorism; the Bahrain Monetary Agency (which became the Central Bank of Bahrain in September 2006) moved quickly to restrict terrorists' ability to transfer funds through Bahrain's financial system. In October 2006, Bahrain joined the U.S. and 23 other countries in a Proliferation Security Initiative interdiction exercise in the Persian Gulf.

U.S. - BAHRAINI RELATIONS

The American Mission Hospital, affiliated with the National Evangelical Church, has operated continuously in Bahrain for more than a century. Bahrain has also been a base for U.S. naval activity in the Gulf since 1947. When Bahrain became independent, the U.S.-Bahrain relationship was formalized with the establishment of diplomatic relations. The U.S. embassy at Manama was opened September 21, 1971, and a resident ambassador was sent in 1974. The Bahraini embassy in Washington, DC, opened in 1977. In October 1991, Amir Isa bin Salman Al Khalifa made a state visit to Washington. In 2001, Amir Hamad bin Isa Al-Khalifa made his first visit to the U.S. after succeeding his father in 1999. He returned to Washington on an official visit in January 2003. King Hamad made an official visit to Washington in November

2004 to meet with President George W. Bush and cabinet-level officials. In January 2008, President Bush made the first visit by a sitting President to Bahrain. King Hamad visited Washington in March 2008.

Bahrain and the United States signed a Defense Cooperation Agreement in October 1991 granting U.S. forces access to Bahraini facilities and ensuring the right to pre-position material for future crises. Bahrain is the headquarters of the U.S. Navy's Fifth Fleet. The U.S. designated Bahrain a Major Non-NATO Ally in October 2001. Bahrain and the United States signed a Free Trade Agreement in 2004.

In: Bahrain and Jordan   ISBN: 978-1-61942-605-4
Editors: K. Buck and T. J. McPherson   © 2012 Nova Science Publishers, Inc.

Chapter 4

JORDAN COUNTRY PROFILE[*]

United States Department of State

Official Name: Hashemite Kingdom of Jordan

Flag of Jordan.

---

[*] This is an edited, reformatted and augmented version of a Bureau of Near Eastern Affairs Profile, dated March 2011.

GEOGRAPHY

Area: 89,342 sq. km. (34,495 sq. mi.).

Cities: *Capital*--Amman (pop. 2.5 million). *Other cities*--az-Zarqa (472,830), Irbid (272,681), al-'Aqaba (107,115).

PEOPLE

Nationality: *Noun and adjective*--Jordanian(s).

Population (2009): 5.97 million.

Religions (2001 census est.): Sunni Muslim 92%, Christian 6%, other 2%.

Languages: Arabic (official), English.

Education (2007, according to Jordan's Department of Statistics): *Literacy*--92.1%.

Health (2007): *Infant mortality rate*--20/1,000. *Life expectancy*--71.6 yrs. male; 74.4 yrs. female.

Ethnic groups: Mostly Arab but small communities of Circassians, Armenians, and Chechens.

Work force (1.8 million, of which 313,000 are registered guest workers): services 34%, manufacturing 20%, public sector 19%, education 12%, health and social services 11%, agriculture 3%.

Unemployment rate (2008): 13% of economically active Jordanians.

GOVERNMENT

Type: Constitutional monarchy.

Independence: May 25, 1946.

Constitution: January 8, 1952.

Branches: *Executive*--King (chief of state), Prime Minister (head of government), Council of Ministers (cabinet).

Legislative--bicameral parliament (appointed upper house known as the Senate, elected lower house).

Judicial--civil, religious, special courts. Suffrage: Universal at 18.

Administrative subdivisions: Twelve governorates--Irbid, Jarash, Ajloun, al-'Aqaba, Madaba, al-Mafraq, az-Zarqa, Amman, al-Balqa, a-Karak, at-Tafilah, and Ma'an.

ECONOMY

Nominal GDP (2009): $21.92 billion.
Annual real growth rate (2009): 3.2%.
Per capita GDP (2009): $4,700.
Natural resources: Phosphate, potash.
Agriculture (3.01% of GDP in 2009): *Products*--citrus, tomatoes, cucumbers, olives, sheep, poultry, stone fruits, strawberries, melons, dairy. *Land*--4.5% arable; 2.5% cultivated. Industry (15.95% of GDP in 2009): *Types*--clothing, phosphate mining, fertilizers, pharmaceuticals, petroleum refining, cement, potash, inorganic chemicals, and light manufacturing.
Trade: *Exports* (2009)--$7.54 billion: garments, fertilizers, potash, phosphates, pharmaceutical prodSucts and vegetables. *Major markets*--India, U.S., Iraq, Saudi Arabia, EU, U.A.E., Syria, Israel. *Imports* (2009)--$16.12 billion: crude petroleum and derivatives, machinery and equipment, vehicles, iron, and cereals. *Major suppliers*--Saudi Arabia (mainly crude oil and derivatives), EU, China, U.S., Egypt, South Korea, Japan, Turkey.
Note: From 1949 to 1967, Jordan administered the West Bank. Since the 1967 war, when Israel took control of this territory, the United States has considered the West Bank to be territory occupied by Israel. The United States believes that the final status of the West Bank can be determined only through negotiations among the concerned parties based on UN Security Council Resolutions 242 and 338.

PEOPLE

Jordanians are Arabs, except for a few small communities of Circassians, Armenians, and Chechens who have adapted to Arab culture. The official language is Arabic, but English is used widely in commerce and government. About 70% of Jordan's population is urban; less than 6% of the rural population is nomadic or semi-nomadic. Approximately 1.7 million registered Palestinian refugees and other displaced persons, including Iraqis, reside in Jordan.

History

The land that became Jordan is part of the richly historical Fertile Crescent region. Around 2000 B.C., Semitic Amorites settled around the Jordan River in the area called Canaan. Subsequent invaders and settlers included Hittites, Egyptians, Israelites, Assyrians, Babylonians, Persians, Greeks, Romans, Arab Muslims, Christian Crusaders, Mameluks, Ottoman Turks, and, finally, the British. At the end of World War I, the League of Nations awarded the territory now comprising Israel, Jordan, the West Bank, Gaza, and Jerusalem to the United Kingdom as the mandate for Palestine and Transjordan. In 1922, the British divided the mandate by establishing the semiautonomous Emirate of Transjordan, ruled by the Hashemite Prince Abdullah, while continuing the administration of Palestine under a British High Commissioner. The mandate over Transjordan ended on May 22, 1946; on May 25, the country became the independent Hashemite Kingdom of Transjordan. It ended its special defense treaty relationship with the United Kingdom in 1957.

Transjordan was one of the Arab states which moved to assist Palestinian nationalists opposed to the creation of Israel in May 1948, and took part in the warfare between the Arab states and the newly founded State of Israel. The armistice agreements of April 3, 1949 left Jordan in control of the West Bank and provided that the armistice demarcation lines were without prejudice to future territorial settlements or boundary lines.

In 1950, the country was renamed the Hashemite Kingdom of Jordan to include those portions of Palestine annexed by King Abdullah I. While recognizing Jordanian administration over the West Bank, the United States maintained the position that ultimate sovereignty was subject to future agreement.

Jordan signed a mutual defense pact in May 1967 with Egypt, and it participated in the June 1967 war between Israel and the Arab states of Syria, Egypt, and Iraq. During the war, Israel gained control of the West Bank and all of Jerusalem. In 1988, Jordan renounced all claims to the West Bank but retained an administrative role pending a final settlement, and its 1994 treaty with Israel allowed for a continuing Jordanian role in Muslim holy places in Jerusalem. The U.S. Government considers the West Bank to be territory occupied by Israel and believes that its final status should be determined through direct negotiations among the parties concerned on the basis of UN Security Council Resolutions 242 and 338.

The 1967 war led to a dramatic increase in the number of Palestinians living in Jordan. Its Palestinian refugee population--700,000 in 1966--grew by another 300,000 from the West Bank. The period following the 1967 war saw an upsurge in the power and importance of Palestinian resistance elements (fedayeen) in Jordan. The heavily armed fedayeen constituted a growing threat to the sovereignty and security of the Hashemite state, and open fighting erupted in September 1970.

No fighting occurred along the 1967 Jordan River cease-fire line during the October 1973 Arab-Israeli war, but Jordan sent a brigade to Syria to fight Israeli units on Syrian territory. Jordan did not participate in the Gulf war of 1990-91. In 1991, Jordan agreed, along with Syria, Lebanon, and Palestinian representatives, to participate in direct peace negotiations with Israel sponsored by the U.S. and Russia. It negotiated an end to hostilities with Israel and signed a peace treaty in 1994. Jordan has since sought to remain at peace with all of its neighbors.

GOVERNMENT

Jordan is a constitutional monarchy based on the constitution promulgated on January 8, 1952. Executive authority is vested in the King and his Council of Ministers. The King signs and executes all laws. His veto power may be overridden by a two-thirds vote of both houses of the parliament. He appoints and may dismiss all judges by decree, approves amendments to the constitution, declares war, and commands the armed forces. Cabinet decisions, court judgments, and the national currency are issued in his name. The King, who may dismiss other cabinet members at the prime minister's request, appoints the council of ministers, led by a prime minister. The cabinet is responsible to the lower house of parliament on matters of general policy and can be forced to resign by a two-thirds vote of "no confidence" by that body. In December 2009, King Abdullah dismissed the cabinet as part of wider effort to strengthen governance and reform in the country. In 2010 and 2011, he again made changes to the cabinet.

Legislative power rests in the bicameral parliament. The lower house of parliament, elected by universal suffrage to a 4-year term, is subject to dissolution by the King. The King appoints the 55-member upper house for a 4-year term. Elections for municipal councils and mayors were held in July 2007; 20% of the council seats were reserved by quota for women. Following November 2007 parliamentary elections, women held seven seats; six seats in the lower house of parliament were reserved by quota for women, and a seventh woman won a seat outside the quota. The King dissolved parliament in November 2009; new elections were held November 9, 2010.

The constitution provides for three categories of courts--civil, religious, and special. Administratively, Jordan is divided into 12 governorates, each headed by a governor appointed by the King. They are the sole authorities for all government departments and development projects in their respective areas.

Principal Government Officials

Chief of State--King Abdullah II ibn Al-Hussein
Prime Minister--Marouf Bakhit
Minister of Defense--Marouf Bakhit
Foreign Minister--Nasser Judeh
Ambassador to the U.S.--Alia Bouran
Ambassador to the UN--Zeid Al-Hussein

Jordan maintains an embassy in the United States at 3504 International Drive NW, Washington, DC 20008 (tel. 202-966-2664).

Political Conditions

King Hussein ruled Jordan from 1953 to 1999, surviving a number of challenges to his rule, drawing on the loyalty of his military, and serving as a symbol of unity and stability for both the East Bank and Palestinian communities in Jordan. In 1989 and 1993, Jordan held free and fair parliamentary elections. Controversial changes in the election law led Islamist parties to boycott the 1997 elections. King Hussein ended martial law in 1991 and legalized political parties in 1992.

King Abdullah II succeeded his father Hussein following the latter's death in February 1999. King Abdullah moved quickly to reaffirm Jordan's peace treaty with Israel and its relations with the U.S., and has since focused the government's agenda on economic reform, political development, and poverty alleviation.

Jordan's continuing structural economic difficulties, burgeoning population, and more open political environment have led to the emergence of a variety of small political parties. In parliamentary elections held November 2007, the Islamist opposition lost many of the seats it had gained in 2003.

In November 2009, the King dissolved parliament. New elections were held November 2010.

Economy

Jordan is a small country with limited natural resources. It is among the most water-poor countries in the world. The country is currently exploring ways to expand its limited water supply and use its existing water resources more efficiently, including through regional cooperation. Jordan also depends on external sources for the majority of its energy requirements. During the 1990s, its crude petroleum needs were met through imports from neighboring Iraq, often at concessionary prices. Since early 2003, Jordan has imported oil primarily from Saudi Arabia at concessionary and market prices. In addition, a natural gas pipeline from Egypt to Jordan through the southern port city of Aqaba is now operational. The pipeline has reached northern Jordan and construction to connect it to Syria and beyond is underway. Jordan developed a new energy strategy in 2007 aiming to develop more indigenous and renewable energy sources, including oil shale, nuclear energy, wind, and solar power.

Under King Abdullah, Jordan has undertaken a program of economic reform. The government has eliminated most fuel and agricultural subsidies, passed legislation targeting corruption, and begun tax reform. It has also worked to liberalize trade, joining the World Trade Organization (WTO) in 2000; signing an Association Agreement with the European Union (EU) in 2001; and signing the first bilateral free trade agreement (FTA) between the U.S. and an Arab country. Under the terms of the U.S.-Jordan FTA, which entered into force in 2001, the United States and Jordan agreed to phased tariff reductions culminating in the complete elimination of duties on nearly all products by 2010. The agreement contains labor and environmental provisions, and also provides for more open markets in communications, construction, finance, health, transportation, and services, as well as the strict application of international standards for the protection of intellectual property. In 1996, the U.S. Congress created Qualifying Industrial Zones (QIZ) to support the peace process. QIZ goods, which must contain a certain percentage of Israeli input and enter the United States tariff- and quota-free, have also driven economic growth, particularly in the export of light manufactured products such as garments. Jordan exported $6.9 million in goods to the U.S. in 1997, when two-way trade was $395 million; according to the U.S. International Trade Commission, it exported $796.2 million in the first 10 months of 2009, with U.S. exports to Jordan valued at $976.9 million and two-way trade reaching $1.77 billion. In 2009, Jordan's economy continued to grow slightly but was hurt by lower than expected revenues and slower growth due to the global financial crisis.

In 1996, Jordan and the United States signed a civil aviation agreement that provides for "open skies" between the two countries, and a U.S.-Jordan Bilateral Investment Treaty (BIT) for the protection and encouragement of bilateral investment entered into force in 2003. The United States and Jordan also signed in 2007 a Science and Technology Cooperation Agreement to facilitate and strengthen scientific cooperation between the two countries, as well as a memorandum of understanding on nuclear energy cooperation. Such agreements bolster efforts to help diversify Jordan's economy and promote growth, and at the same time lessen reliance on exports of phosphates, potash, and recently textiles; overseas remittances; and foreign aid. The government has emphasized the information technology (IT), pharmaceuticals, and tourism sectors as other promising growth sectors. The low tax and low regulation Aqaba Special Economic Zone (ASEZ) is considered a model of a government-provided framework for private sector-led economic growth.

Jordan is classified by the World Bank as a "lower middle income country." The per capita GDP is $4,700. According to Jordan's Department of Statistics, almost 13% of the economically active Jordanian population residing in Jordan was unemployed in 2008, although unofficial estimates cite a 30% unemployment rate. Education and literacy rates and measures of social well-being are relatively high compared to other countries with similar incomes. Jordan's population growth rate has declined in recent years and is currently 2.3% as reported by the Jordanian Government. One of the most important factors in the government's efforts to improve the well-being of its citizens is the macroeconomic stability that has been achieved since the 1990s. Jordan's 2008 and 2009 budgets emphasized increases in the social safety net to help people most impacted by high inflation, but these increases were not included in the 2010 budget because of fiscal austerity plans and the low inflation rates during 2009. The average rate of inflation in 2009 was -0.1%. The currency has been stable with an exchange rate fixed to the U.S. dollar since 1995 at JD 0.708 to the dollar. In 2008, Jordan participated in a Paris Club debt buyback to retire more than $2 billion in debt using privatization proceeds which, at the time, reduced the percentage of external debt to GDP from 46% to 32%.

While pursuing economic reform and increased trade, Jordan's economy will continue to be vulnerable to external shocks and regional unrest. Without calm in the region, economic growth seems destined to stay below its potential. Jordan's conservative banking sector was largely protected from the worldwide financial crisis but many businesses, particularly in the tourism and real estate sector, experienced a slowdown in 2009.

FOREIGN RELATIONS

Jordan has consistently followed a pro-Western foreign policy and traditionally has had close relations with the United States. These relations were damaged by support in Jordan for Iraq during the first Gulf war (1990-91). Although the Government of Jordan stated its opposition to the Iraqi occupation of Kuwait, popular support for Iraq was driven by Jordan's Palestinian community, which favored Saddam as a champion against Western supporters of Israel.

Following the first Gulf war, Jordan largely restored its relations with Western countries through its participation in the Middle East peace process and enforcement of UN sanctions against Iraq. Relations between Jordan and the Gulf countries improved substantially after King Hussein's death. Since the 2003 fall of the Iraqi regime, Jordan has played a pivotal role in supporting the restoration of stability and security to Iraq. The Government of Jordan has facilitated the training of over 50,000 Iraqi police cadets and corrections officers at a Jordanian facility near Amman. Jordan also plays host to a significant Iraqi population and has worked closely with donor agencies and the international community to address their humanitarian needs. In 2008, Jordan appointed and sent an ambassador to Iraq in an effort to strengthen bilateral ties.

Jordan signed a nonbelligerency agreement with Israel (the Washington Declaration) in Washington, DC, on July 25, 1994. Jordan and Israel signed a historic peace treaty on October 26, 1994, witnessed by President Bill Clinton. The U.S. has participated with Jordan and Israel in trilateral development discussions in which key issues have been water-sharing and security; cooperation on Jordan Rift Valley development; infrastructure projects; and trade, finance, and banking issues. Jordan also participates in multilateral peace talks. Jordan belongs to the UN and several of its specialized and related agencies, including the World Trade Organization (WTO), the International Meteorological Organization (IMO), Food and Agriculture Organization

(FAO), International Atomic Energy Agency (IAEA), International Civil Aviation Organization (ICAO), and World Health Organization (WHO). Jordan also is a member of the World Bank, International Monetary Fund (IMF), Organization of the Islamic Conference (OIC), Nonaligned Movement, and Arab League.

Since the outbreak of the second Intifada in September 2000, Jordan has worked to maintain lines of communication between the Israelis and the Palestinians to counsel moderation and to return the parties to negotiations of outstanding permanent status issues. These efforts bore fruit with the resumption of Israeli-Palestinian peace negotiations at the November 2007 Annapolis conference. Jordan has played an important role in facilitating the peace process through the training of several thousand Palestinian security force personnel.

U.S.-JORDANIAN RELATIONS

Relations between the United States and Jordan have been close for 6 decades, with 2009 marking the 60th anniversary of U.S.-Jordanian ties. A primary objective of U.S. policy has been the achievement of a comprehensive, just, and lasting peace in the Middle East.

U.S. policy seeks to reinforce Jordan's commitment to peace, stability, and moderation. The peace process and Jordan's opposition to terrorism parallel and indirectly assist wider U.S. interests. Accordingly, through economic and military assistance and through close political cooperation, the United States has helped Jordan maintain its stability and prosperity.

Since 1952 the United States has worked closely with Jordan to improve the lives of Jordanian citizens. Development assistance totaling nearly $6 billion has resulted in dramatically improved health indicators, road and water networks, hundreds of schools built, thousands of Jordanians in critical fields educated and trained in the U.S., and grants and loans for U.S. agricultural commodities. Current focus areas include education, access to water, resource management and conservation, energy, youth and poverty alleviation programs, maternal/child health, energy, governance, macroeconomic policy, workforce development, and competitiveness. These programs are an essential contributor to a strong bilateral relationship centered on a stable, reform-oriented Jordan. Jordan signed a Threshold Agreement with the Millennium Challenge Corporation (MCC) in October 2006, and was subsequently deemed by the MCC to be eligible for a Compact Agreement in recognition of the country's progress on economic, social, and political reform indicators. A strong U.S. military assistance program is designed to meet Jordan's legitimate defense needs, including preservation of border integrity and regional stability through the provision of materiel and training. In 2008, the U.S. and Jordan signed a non-binding memorandum of understanding (MOU) to provide assistance to Jordan over a 5-year period, subject to the appropriation and availability of funds for this purpose. The MOU also reinforces the commitment to broaden cooperation and dialogue in a variety of areas.

INDEX